The Organizational Change Management Communications Playbook

How To Achieve Success and Avoid Failure

Best Practice Guides for Best Practices To Planning,
Transformation, Technology, and Innovation.

Ken Martin

Ken Martin

Copyright

Copyright © 2023 by 3 Magic Publications

Dedication

This book is dedicated to my amazing twin boys Jack and Jake.

Contents

Contents

Preface

I have always been interested in effective communications and the art of making the complex simple. This approach is the primary goal of 3 Magic Publications, which I founded to facilitate successful business change and transformation by using innovative and creative documentation to communicate key messages and best practices.

During my career, I wanted a reference method of best practices at my fingertips, where, instead of reading numerous self-development, management, and technical books, I could have a handy one-page cheat sheet. So, I developed "One Page Magic," the idea of having one book on a page, which has evolved into this new table format. I hope you find these best practice guides useful for your continued success in your career.

Ken Martin

"BEWARE OF FALSE KNOWLEDGE; IT IS
MORE DANGEROUS THAN IGNORANCE."

George Bernard Shaw

Introduction

How to read

The Organization Change Management Communications Playbook comprises hands-on experience and best practices that cover all aspects of planning and implementing a successful change program that offers sustainable results.

Important note

Many change activities are duplicated across a change program. All these duplicated activities have been included for completeness in this guide.

One significant benefit of the one-page planning process is that all these repeated activities are visible to avoid duplication of efforts and enable team members to leverage the work of other team members in the change program. Another benefit is that these activities, even when duplicated, are not missed altogether, which is a common occurrence in change programs and often the cause of limiting success or total failure.

Why use best practices?

There is a well-known phrase: "Keeping doing the same thing and expecting different results is a sign of insanity." Yet this is what many people and companies continue to do by doing the same things, making the same mistakes, and expecting different results. But how many professionals have recorded lessons learned, and even more rarely, how many professionals have read lessons learned from others' experiences of previous projects?

Best practices often derived from lessons learned and hard-earned experience can save you a lot of wasted effort, time, and often failure. They can contribute to your success in all aspects of your career and life. Learn from others' best practice experiences, avoid common mistakes, and succeed for the first time.

OCM Communications

To implement a change program, the following key activities should be considered:

- Clearly define the change that needs to be implemented and the business case for it.
- Assemble a team of people from different departments and levels of the organization who will be impacted by the
- Develop a shared vision for a change that is aligned with the organization's overall goals and objectives.
- Create a plan that includes specific milestones and deliverables, as well as a schedule for delivering them.
- Communicate the plan to all stakeholders, including the team, management, and employees who will be impacted by the change.

- Regularly monitor progress and make adjustments as needed.
- Continuously involve stakeholders, such as customers and end-users, to gather feedback and ensure that the change is meeting their needs.
- Celebrate successes along the way to keep the team motivated and on track.
- Continuously adapt the plan as needed to ensure that the change is meeting the organization's goals and objectives.
- Monitor and sustain the change to ensure that it continues to deliver value to the firm.

It's important to keep in mind to keep the change approach flexible and adaptable so these activities may need to be adjusted depending on the specific change program being implemented.

The Five Success Factors for Change

The five key success factors for organizational change management are as follows:

1. Strong and effective leadership is essential for driving change and gaining buy-in from employees and other stakeholders.
2. A clear vision and plan for the change, including specific goals and milestones, can help to keep the change on track and ensure that it is implemented successfully.
3. Clear and transparent communication throughout the change process is necessary so that all stakeholders understand the reasons for change and their role in the process.
4. Staff are more likely to support and embrace change when they feel that they are part of the process and that their opinions and ideas are valued.
5. The change should be aligned with the business strategy and goals, so that it is clear how the change will contribute to the firm's success.

The ability to adapt and adjust to changing circumstances is critical for successful change management, as there will often be unanticipated challenges and obstacles that arise during the process.

Employees need to be trained and provided with the necessary support to adapt to the changes.

The change process should be monitored and evaluated to ensure that it is on track and to make adjustments if necessary.

1. Change success factor - leadership

Communicate the need for change	Clearly communicate the need for change and the vision for the future state.
Involve stakeholders in the change process	Involve key stakeholders in the planning and implementation process.
Create a detailed & realistic plan	Create a comprehensive and realistic plan for implementing the change.
Staff training & support	Provide training and support for employees to help them adapt to the new changes.
Monitor progress	Monitor progress and make adjustments as needed.
Communicate regularly with employees	Communicate regularly with employees to address concerns and provide updates.
Lead by example & show commitment	Lead by example and demonstrate a commitment to the change.
Encourage employee participation	Encourage and recognize employee participation and contributions to the change effort.
A culture of continual improvement	Foster a culture of continuous improvement to sustain the changes over time.
Prepare for resistance to change	Be prepared to handle resistance to change and have a plan in place to address it.

2. Change success factor - vision

Clearly define the goals and objectives	Clearly define the goals and objectives of the change program and how they align with the I strategy of the firm.
Develop a detailed plan	Develop a detailed plan that outlines the steps needed to achieve the desired outcome &timelines and milestones.
Communicate the vision and plan	Communicate the vision and plan to all stakeholders (staff, customers) that aligns with their needs and concerns.
Be flexible and open	Be flexible and open to adjusting the plan as needed based on feedback and changes in the business environment.
Identify and address potential obstacles	Identify and address potential obstacles and challenges that may arise during the implementation process.
Monitor progress and measure success	Monitor progress and measure success so the plan stays on track to achieve the desired outcome.
Communicate the progress & the impact	Communicate the progress & the impact of the change to all stakeholders regularly so everyone is aware of the progress.
Engage and empower stakeholders	Engage and empower stakeholders to actively participate in the change process & make sure they understand their role
The plan supports the firm's overall strategy	Ensure that the plan supports the firm's overall strategy and goals, and aligns with the organization's culture and values.
Continuously evaluate the plan	Continuously evaluate the plan, measure progress and adjust as necessary so it achieves the desired outcome.

3. Change success factor - comms

Develop a clear and consistent comms plan	Develop a clear and consistent comms plan that outlines the message, target audience, and the communication channels.
Communicate the change early & often	Communicate the change early and often, providing regular updates on progress & addressing any concerns.
Tailor the message and communications	Tailor the message and communication approach to different stakeholders, such as employees, customers, and partners.
Use multiple channels of communication	Use multiple channels of communication (face-to-face meetings, email, newsletters) to reach a wide audience.
Involve stakeholders in the comms process	Involve key stakeholders in the communication process to build buy-in and support for the change.
Communicate the benefits of the change	Communicate the benefits of the change and how it aligns with the organization's overall strategy and goals.
Provide training and support to employees	Provide training and support to help employees understand and adapt to the changes.
Address and manage resistance to change	Address and manage resistance to change by addressing concerns and providing solutions.
Encourage two-way communication	Encourage two-way communication and provide opportunities for employees to give feedback and ask questions.
Continuously evaluate the comms plan	Continuously evaluate the comms plan and adjust as needed to ensure that all stakeholders

4. Success factor for change - employees

Involve staff in the planning	Involve staff in the planning and implementation process from the very beginning with focus groups, surveys, or interviews.
Communicate the change & its rationale	Communicate the change and its rationale clearly and honestly to all employees.
Provide staff with training & support	Provide employees with the necessary training and support to adapt to the changes.
Encourage employee participation	Encourage employee participation and contributions throughout the change process.
Empower employees to take ownership	Empower employees to take ownership of the change by assigning them specific roles and responsibilities.
Create time for staff to give feedback	Create opportunities for employees to give feedback and ask questions.
Recognize and reward employees	Recognize and reward employees for their contributions to the change effort.
Address and manage resistance	Address and manage resistance to change by addressing concerns and providing solutions.
A culture of continual improvement	Foster a culture of continuous improvement to sustain the changes over time.
Evaluate the staff involvement	Continuously evaluate the staff involvement strategy and adjust as needed so that all staff are engaged & committed.

5. Change success factor - alignment

Clearly defining the change	Before any changes are made, it's important to have a clear understanding of what the change entails, why it's necessary, and what the desired outcome is.
Align the change with the firm's mission, vision, and goals	The proposed change should be aligned with the overall mission, vision, and goals of the organization. This will ensure that the change is in line with the organization's overall strategy and direction.
Involving key stakeholders	It's important to involve key stakeholders in the change process, such as employees, customers, and suppliers. This will ensure that their concerns and feedback are taken into account and that they are more likely to support the change.
Communicating the change effectively	Clear and effective communication is crucial for ensuring that employees understand the change and its rationale.
Providing training and support	Providing training and support to employees during the change process can help them adjust to the change and be more successful in their new roles.
Measuring and monitoring progress	Measuring and monitoring progress throughout the change process can help to identify any issues and make adjustments as needed. This will ensure that the change is successful and that the desired outcome is achieved.
Continuously evaluating the change	Continuously evaluating the change after implementation will help ensure that it is meeting the desired outcome, and that the organization's mission, vision and goals are being met.

Tools to facilitate change management

General overview	There are several tools that can be used to facilitate change and ensure the change process is well-planned, and well-managed to achieve the desired outcomes.
Change management methodology	A structured change management methodology, such as Lewin's Change Management Model or Kotter's 8-Step Change Model, can be used to guide the change process.
Communication plans	Developing a communication plan can help ensure that all stakeholders are informed about the change and its rationale.
Training and development	Providing training & development opportunities can help staff acquire the skills & knowledge to adjust to the change.
Project management tools	Project management tools, such as Gantt charts and project timelines, can be used to plan, organize, and track progress.
Performance metrics	Performance metrics can be used to measure the success of the change and identify needed areas of improvements.
Employee engagement survey	Staff engagement survey can be conducted to assess their attitude and involvement in the change process.
Stakeholder analysis	Conducting a stakeholder analysis can help identify key stakeholders and assess their level of support for the change.
Risk management	Identifying potential risks and developing a plan to mitigate them can help ensure the success of the change.
Change management software	There are various change management software available to help manage, track, and report on the progress of changes.
Acknowledgement	**All trademarks are acknowledged.**

"A ROOM WITHOUT BOOKS IS LIKE A BODY WITHOUT A SOUL."

Cicero

The One Page Planning Process

The one-page planning is a simple and effective planning & governance process for projects and programs.

Once this simple process is set up it is very effective, it continually shows the big picture, highlights accountability and gains engagement and buy-in from the teams and stakeholders.

The strategic PMO program's workstreams (subprojects) are all listed in the one-page master plan, which also specifies the changes that must be implemented and when. Each workstream needs to have specific goals, benchmarks, parameters, timetables, and financial constraints.

One Page Planning Linkages:

This diagram on the next page shows the linkages between the master one-page plan and a work-stream one page plan with clear accountabilities.

The Master One Page Plan:

The master one-page plan usually owned by a program manager provides an overview of all work-streams for reporting with a project manager assigned as owner to each work stream.

The Workstream One Page Plans:

The workstream one page plans feed into the master one-page plan as supporting workstreams. Work-stream support plans are typically owned by a project manager but the work-streams in those work-stream plans can be assigned owners to SMEs and impacted or interested stakeholders.

Implementing change is difficult...

Implementing a sustainable change within an organisation can be a very difficult task. People don't alter their characteristics or how they perceive the world just because leadership decides a change would be beneficial to the firm.

Having the right people with the right skill sets and an effective change plan are both critical success factors for a successful strategic change program.

The Master Plan Overview

The one-page planning master program management plan is a document that outlines the process for managing the whole program. A comprehensive plan defines the key success areas of the program that capture the scope, objectives, and deliverables of the program, as well as the resources, budget, and timeline required to complete the program. The plan also outlines the roles and responsibilities of the program team, as well as the process for managing risks, issues, and stakeholders.

The purpose of the master plan is to provide a clear, concise, and consistent approach and the overall status of the program. It helps to ensure that the program stays on track, stays within budget, and delivers the desired results. The master one-page plan provides an important tool for communication, coordination, accountability and control which is essential for the successful delivery of a program.

This simple approach, along with supporting workstreams, helps to establish clear ownership and accountability for each key focus area of the program. This will help ensure that progress is made and that any challenges or issues are quickly addressed. This is a visible benefit of using the one-page planning process.

These workstreams are typically managed by an individual project manager and they are coordinated by the program manager, who is responsible for ensuring that all the necessary activities are completed and that the program is delivered successfully.

Starting an organisational change program can be a difficult process and it is important to approach it carefully to ensure the best chances of success.

One Page Plan Linkages

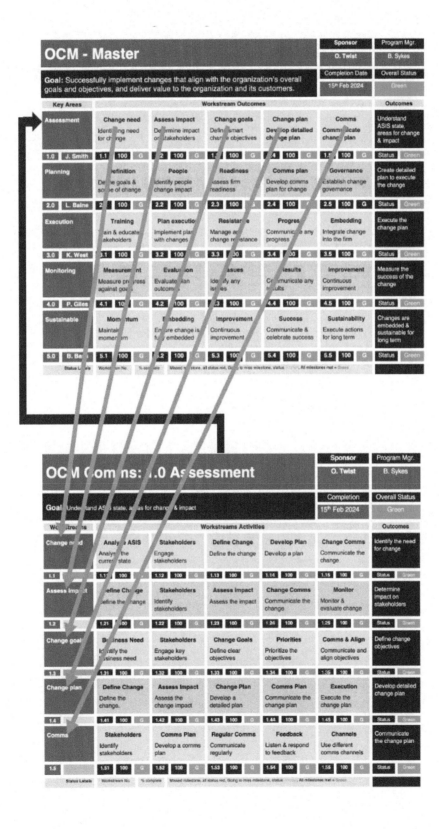

OCM Comms - Master

OCM - Master

	Sponsor	Program Mgr.
	O. Twist	B. Sykes
	Completion Date	Overall Status
	15th Feb 2024	Green

Goal: Successfully implement changes that align with the organization's overall goals and objectives, and deliver value to the organization and its customers.

Key Areas	Workstream Outcomes					Outcomes
Assessment	**Change need** Identifying need for change	**Assess impact** Determine impact on stakeholders	**Change goals** Define smart change objectives	**Change plan** Develop detailed change plan	**Comms** Communicate change plan	Understand ASIS state, areas for change & impact
1.0 J. Smith	**1.1** 100 G	**1.2** 100 G	**1.3** 100 G	**1.4** 100 G	**1.5** 100 G	Status Green
Planning	**Definition** Define goals & scope of change	**People** Identify people change impact	**Readiness** Assess firm readiness	**Comms plan** Develop comms plan for change	**Governance** Establish change governance	Create detailed plan to execute the change
2.0 L. Baine	**2.1** 100 G	**2.2** 100 G	**2.3** 100 G	**2.4** 100 G	**2.5** 100 G	Status Green
Execution	**Training** Train & educate stakeholders	**Plan execution** Implement plan with changes	**Resistance** Manage any change resistance	**Progress** Communicate any progress	**Embedding** Integrate change into the firm	Execute the change plan
3.0 K. West	**3.1** 100 G	**3.2** 100 G	**3.3** 100 G	**3.4** 100 G	**3.5** 100 G	Status Green
Monitoring	**Measurement** Measure progress against goals	**Evaluation** Evaluate plan outcomes	**Issues** Identify any issues	**Results** Communicate any results	**Improvement** Continuous improvement	Measure the success of the change
4.0 P. Giles	**4.1** 100 G	**4.2** 100 G	**4.3** 100 G	**4.4** 100 G	**4.5** 100 G	Status Green
Sustainable	**Momentum** Maintain momentum	**Embedding** Ensure change is fully embedded	**Improvement** Continuous improvement	**Success** Communicate & celebrate success	**Sustainability** Execute actions for long term	Changes are embedded & sustainable for long term
5.0 B. Bass	**5.1** 100 G	**5.2** 100 G	**5.3** 100 G	**5.4** 100 G	**5.5** 100 G	Status Green

Status Labels	Workstream No.	% complete	Missed milestone, all status red, Going to miss milestone, status orange, All milestones met = Green

1.0 Assessment Workstream Plan

OCM Comms: 1.0 Assessment						Sponsor	Program Mgr.
						O. Twist	B. Sykes
Goal: Understand ASIS state, areas for change & impact						Completion	Overall Status
						15th Feb 2024	Green

Workstreams	Workstreams Activities					Outcomes
Change need	**Analyse ASIS** Analyse the current state	**Stakeholders** Engage stakeholders	**Define Change** Define the change	**Develop Plan** Develop a plan	**Change Comms** Communicate the change	Identify the need for change
1.1	1.11 100 G	1.12 100 G	1.13 100 G	1.14 100 G	1.15 100 G	Status Green
Assess impact	**Define Change** Define the change	**Stakeholders** Identify stakeholders	**Assess impact** Assess the impact	**Change Comms** Communicate the change	**Monitor** Monitor & evaluate change	Determine impact on stakeholders
1.2	1.21 100 G	1.22 100 G	1.23 100 G	1.24 100 G	1.25 100 G	Status Green
Change goals	**Business Need** Identify the business need	**Stakeholders** Engage key stakeholders	**Change Goals** Define clear objectives	**Priorities** Prioritize the objectives	**Comms & Align** Communicate and align objectives	Define change objectives
1.3	1.31 100 G	1.32 100 G	1.33 100 G	1.34 100 G	1.35 100 G	Status Green
Change plan	**Define Change** Define the change.	**Assess Impact** Assess the change impact	**Change Plan** Develop a detailed plan	**Comms Plan** Communicate the change plan	**Execution** Execute the change plan	Develop detailed change plan
1.4	1.41 100 G	1.42 100 G	1.43 100 G	1.44 100 G	1.45 100 G	Status Green
Comms	**Stakeholders** Identify stakeholders	**Comms Plan** Develop a comms plan	**Regular Comms** Communicate regularly	**Feedback** Listen & respond to feedback	**Channels** Use different comms channels	Communicate the change plan
1.5	1.51 100 G	1.52 100 G	1.53 100 G	1.54 100 G	1.55 100 G	Status Green
Status Labels	Workstream No.	% complete	Missed milestone, all status red, Going to miss milestone, status orange, All milestones met = Green			

2.0 Planning Workstream Plan

OCM Comms: 2.0 Planning					Program Mgr.	Project Mgr.
					B. Sykes	L. Baines
Goal: Create detailed plan to execute the change.					Completion Date	Overall Status
					15th Feb 2024	Green

Definitions	Need for Change	Assess ASIS	Define TOBE	Change Plan	Comms Change	Create detailed plan to execute the change
	Identify the need for change	Assess the current state	Define the future state	Develop a change plan	Communicate & execute change	
2.1	2.11 100 G	2.12 100 G	2.13 100 G	2.14 100 G	2.15 100 G	Status Green
People	Identification	Analysis	Stakeholder Map	Engagement	Communications	Identify people change impact
	Identify all the stakeholders	Analyse the stakeholders	Create a map of stakeholders	Engage with stakeholders	Communicate with stakeholders	
2.2	2.21 100 G	2.22 100 G	2.23 100 G	2.24 100 G	2.25 100 G	Status Green
Readiness	Capabilities	Gaps	Culture	Resistance	Change Team	Assess firm readiness
	Asses ASIS capabilities	Identify gaps	Assess firm's culture	Assess change resistance	Identify & assemble team	
2.3	2.31 100 G	2.32 100 G	2.33 100 G	2.34 100 G	2.35 100 G	Status Green
Comms Plan	Stakeholders	Comms Strategy	Messaging	Schedule	Evaluation	Develop comms plan for change
	Identify key stakeholders	Develop a comms strategy	Create clear messaging	Create a comms schedule	Evaluate & adjust comms plan	
2.4	2.41 100 G	2.42 100 G	2.43 100 G	2.44 100 G	2.45 100 G	Status Green
Governance	Team	Roles	Decisions	Metrics	Reviews	Establish a governance structure
	Establish a governance team	Define roles & responsibilities	Develop decision-making process	Create metrics for performance	Regularly review governance	
2.5	2.51 100 2.5	2.52 100 G	2.53 100 G	2.54 100 G	2.55 100 G	Status Green

Status Labels	Workstream No.	% complete	Missed milestone, all status red, Going to miss milestone, status , All milestones met = Green			

3.0 Execution Workstream Plan

OCM Comms: 3.0 Execution						Program Mgr.	Project Mgr.
Goal: Put developed plan into action.						B. Sykes	K.West
						Completion	Overall Status
						15th Feb 2024	Green

Training	**Vision & Goals** Communicate the vision & goals	**Training** Provide training to stakeholders	**Collaboration** Create a culture of collaboration	**Ongoing Support** Provide ongoing support	**Measurement** Measure & report change progress	Train & educate stakeholders
3.1	3.11 100 G	3.12 100 G	3.13 100 G	3.14 100 G	3.15 100 G	Status Green
Execute plan	**Develop plan** Develop a detailed plan	**Prioritisation** Define & prioritise work	**Teams** Form teams and assign roles	**Execution** Execute & monitor the plan	**Evaluation** Evaluate the outcome	Execute the change plan
3.2	3.21 100 G	3.22 100 G	3.23 100 G	3.24 100 G	3.25 100 G	Status Green
Resistance	**Identification** Understand the resistance	**Change Benefits** Communicate the change benefits	**Involvement** Involve stake-holders in process	**Transition** Support during transition	**Issues** Address & resolve any issues	Manage any change resistance
3.3	3.31 100 G	3.32 100 G	3.33 100 G	3.34 100 G	3.35 100 G	Status Green
Progress	**Comms Plan** Establish a comms plan	**Updates** Provide regular updates	**Channels** Use multiple comms channels	**Success** Communicate success	**Feedback** Gather feedback & address issues	Communicate any progress
3.4	3.41 100 G	3.42 100 G	3.43 100 G	3.44 100 G	3.45 100 G	Status Green
Embedding	**Accountability** Establish clear accountability	**Incorporation** Incorporate the change into BAU	**Celebration** Celebrate the change	**Monitoring** Monitor progress & adjust as need	**Capability** Build in-house capability	Integrate change into the firm
3.5	3.51 100 G	3.52 100 G	3.53 100 G	3.54 100 G	3.55 100 G	Status Green

| Status Labels | Workstream No. | % complete | One red, then status red, One orange, then status | , All green = Complete | |

4.0 Monitoring Workstream Plan

OCM Comms: 4.0 Monitoring					Program Mgr.	Project Mgr.
Goal: Measure the success of the change.					B. Sykes	**P. Giles**
					Completion	Overall Status
					15th Feb 2024	Green
Measurement	**Metrics & KPIs** Establish metrics & KPIs	**Collect Data** Regularly collect & analyse data	**Progress** Communicate progress & results	**Issues** Identify & address any issues	**Assessment** Continually assess & adjust	Measure progress against goals
4.1	4.11 · 100 · G	4.12 · 100 · G	4.13 · 100 · G	4.14 · 100 · G	4.15 · 100 · G	Status · Green
Evaluation	**Criteria** Define evaluation criteria	**Collect Data** Collect & analyse data	**Success** Assess program's success	**Results** Communicate evaluation results	**Findings** Include finding into decisions	Evaluate plan outcomes
4.2	4.21 · 100 · G	4.22 · 100 · G	4.23 · 100 · G	4.24 · 100 · G	4.25 · 100 · G	Status · Green
Issues	**Progress** Regularly monitor progress	**Open Comms** Encourage open communications	**Check-ins** Conduct regular check-ins	**Analysis** Analyse data and metrics	**Risk Register** Establish a risk register	Identify any issues
4.3	4.31 · 100 · G	4.32 · 100 · G	4.33 · 100 · G	4.34 · 100 · G	4.35 · 100 · G	Status · Green
Results	**Stakeholders** Identify key stakeholders	**Comms Plan** Develop a comms plan	**Updates** Regularly update stakeholders	**Results** Comm results & outcomes	**Feedback** Encourage feedback	Communicate any results
4.4	4.41 · 100 · G	4.42 · 100 · G	4.43 · 100 · G	4.44 · 100 · G	4.45 · 100 · G	Status · Green
Improvement	**Reviews** Review & analyse results	**Feedback** Establish a feedback process	**Changes** Identify changes based on results	**Progress** Continuously monitor progress	**Alignment** Align processes to best practices	Continuous improvement
4.5	4.51 · 100 · G	4.52 · 100 · G	4.53 · 100 · G	4.54 · 100 · G	4.55 · 100 · G	Status · Green
Status Labels	Workstream No.	% complete	One red, then status red, One orange, then status orange, All green = Complete			

5.0 Sustainable Workstream Plan

OCM Comms: 5.0 Sustainable						Program Mgr.	Project Mgr.
Goal: Changes are embedded & sustainable for long term.						B. Sykes	**B. Bass**
						Completion	Overall Status
						15th Feb 2024	Green
Momentum	**Comms** Communicate regularly	**Monitor** Monitor & track progress	**Training** Provide ongoing training	**Resistance** Address any resistance	**Evaluate** Continuously evaluate	Maintain momentum	
5.1	5.11 100 G	5.12 100 G	5.13 100 G	5.14 100 G	= 100 G	Status	Green
Embedding	**Embedding Plan** Create a plan for embedding	**Improvement** Create a culture of improvement	**Channels** Use a variety of comms channels	**Monitor** Assign resources to monitor	**Metrics** Measure the change outcome	Ensure change is fully embedded	
5.2	5.21 100 G	5.22 100 G	5.23 100 G	5.24 100 G	5.25 100 G	Status	Green
Improvement	**Goals & Metrics** Establish clear goals & metrics	**Feedback Loop** Create a feedback loop.	**Reviews** Regularly assess the change	**Engagement** Support staff involvement	**Data Analysis** Use data analysis & metrics	Continuous improvement	
5.3	5.31 100 G	5.32 100 G	5.33 100 G	5.34 100 G	5.35 100 G	Status	Green
Success	**Comms** Communicate regularly	**Successes** Share successes & progress	**Milestones** Recognize milestones	**Storytelling** Use storytelling & case studies	**Benefits** Communicate the benefits	Communicate & celebrate success	
5.4	5.41 100 G	5.42 100 G	5.43 100 G	5.44 100 G	5.45 100 G	Status	Green
Sustainability	**Measurement** Measure the change	**Risks** Identify & mitigate the risks	**Embed Plan** Develop an embed plan	**Evaluation** Evaluate & adapt change program	**Resilience** Build change-resilient firm	Execute actions for long term	
5.5	5.51 100 G	5.52 100 G	5.53 100 G	5.54 100 G	5.55 100 G	Status	Green
Status Labels	Workstream No.	% complete	One red, then status red, One orange, then status	, All green = Complete			

Ken Martin

MAY YOU ALWAYS KEEP YOUR YOUTH.

Mark Twain

1.0 Assessment

The primary goal of the assessment phase in a change management program is to understand the current state of the organization and identify areas that need to be improved or changed. This includes identifying stakeholders, assessing the current processes and systems in place, and understanding the impact of the proposed changes on the organization as a whole. The information gathered during this phase is used to develop a plan for implementing the changes and to measure the success of the change management program.

The 5 key components and associated activities for the assessment phase for the change management program?

1. Identify the need for change by identifying a problem that requires a change in the current process or system.

2. Determine the potential impact of the change on various stakeholders, including employees, customers, and the organization as a whole.

3. Establish clear and measurable objectives for the change program.

4. Create a detailed plan for implementing the change, including tasks, timelines, and resource needs.

5. Communicate and gain buy-in for the change program to stakeholders and gaining their buy-in for the plan.

1.0 Assessment Plan Linkages

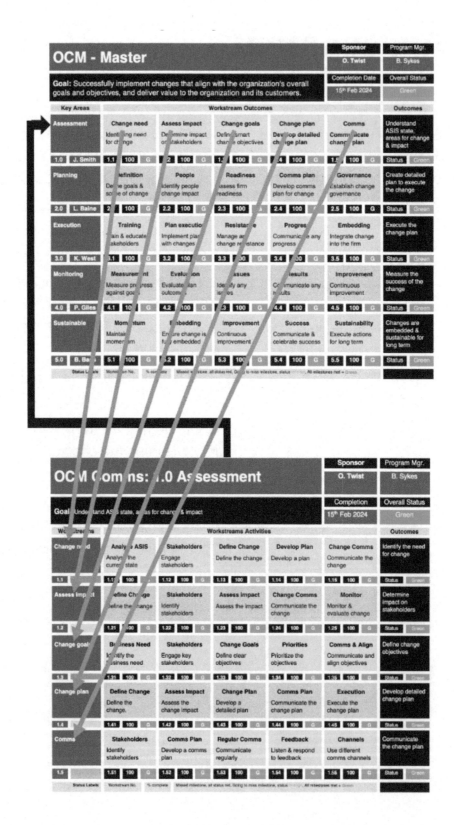

1.0 Assessment Workstream Plan

OCM Comms: 1.0 Assessment						Sponsor	Program Mgr.
						O. Twist	B. Sykes
Goal: Understand ASIS state, areas for change & impact						Completion	Overall Status
						15th Feb 2024	Green

Workstreams	Workstreams Activities					Outcomes
Change need	**Analyse ASIS** Analyse the current state	**Stakeholders** Engage stakeholders	**Define Change** Define the change	**Develop Plan** Develop a plan	**Change Comms** Communicate the change	Identify the need for change
1.1	1.11 100 G	1.12 100 G	1.13 100 G	1.14 100 G	1.15 100 G	Status Green
Assess impact	**Define Change** Define the change	**Stakeholders** Identify stakeholders	**Assess impact** Assess the impact	**Change Comms** Communicate the change	**Monitor** Monitor & evaluate change	Determine impact on stakeholders
1.2	1.21 100 G	1.22 100 G	1.23 100 G	1.24 100 G	1.25 100 G	Status Green
Change goals	**Business Need** Identify the business need	**Stakeholders** Engage key stakeholders	**Change Goals** Define clear objectives	**Priorities** Prioritize the objectives	**Comms & Align** Communicate and align objectives	Define change objectives
1.3	1.31 100 G	1.32 100 G	1.33 100 G	1.34 100 G	1.35 100 G	Status Green
Change plan	**Define Change** Define the change.	**Assess Impact** Assess the change impact	**Change Plan** Develop a detailed plan	**Comms Plan** Communicate the change plan	**Execution** Execute the change plan	Develop detailed change plan
1.4	1.41 100 G	1.42 100 G	1.43 100 G	1.44 100 G	1.45 100 G	Status Green
Comms	**Stakeholders** Identify stakeholders	**Comms Plan** Develop a comms plan	**Regular Comms** Communicate regularly	**Feedback** Listen & respond to feedback	**Channels** Use different comms channels	Communicate the change plan
1.5	1.51 100 G	1.52 100 G	1.53 100 G	1.54 100 G	1.55 100 G	Status Green
Status Labels	Workstream No.	% complete	Missed milestone, all status red, Going to miss milestone, status orange, All milestones met = Green			

1.1 Change Need

The purpose of identifying a problem or opportunity that requires a change in the current process or system is to improve the overall effectiveness and efficiency of the organization. The goals of this process are to:

- Understand the current state of the organization and identify areas for improvement

- Identify the root cause of the problem or opportunity

- *Develop a clear and measurable plan for addressing the issue

- Implement the plan and monitor progress to ensure that the desired changes are achieved.

- Continuously monitor, evaluate and improve the system to adapt to changes in the environment.

If the purpose and goals to identify the problem or opportunity that requires a change in the current process or system are not done effectively or efficiently, it can have several negative impacts on the organization.

Some potential negative impacts include:

- Lack of buy-in from employees, resulting in resistance to change and difficulty in implementing new processes or systems.

- Inefficient allocation of resources, including time, money and personnel.

- Failure to address the root cause of the problem or opportunity, resulting in a lack of sustainable improvements.

- Poorly designed or implemented changes can lead to further problems, or even make the original problem worse.

- Failure to effectively communicate the changes to employees, stakeholders and customers can result in confusion and disruption to business operations.

- Lack of monitoring and evaluation may prevent the organization from identifying issues and course-correcting as needed.

Overall, not effectively identifying the problem or opportunity that requires a change in the current process or system can lead to a significant loss of resources and opportunities for the firm.

1.1 Change need activities

Analyse ASIS	**Analyse the current state.**
	Understand the current processes, systems, and structures in place and identify any pain points or areas for improvement.
Stakeholders	**Engage stakeholders.**
	Gather input and feedback from stakeholders (employees, customers & partners to understand needs and expectations.
Define change	**Define the change.**
	Clearly define the scope & objectives of the change plus the specific problem or opportunity that the change is addressing.
Develop plan	**Develop a plan.**
	Create a detailed plan for implementing the change, including timelines, resources, and responsibilities.
Change comms	**Communicate the change.**
	Communicate the change to all stakeholders (employees, customers, and partners so that everyone understands the rationale for the change and how it will affect them.
Change need outcome	**Identify the need for change.**
	Identify the problem or opportunity that requires a change in the current process or system.

1.1 Change need questions

General overview	There are several key questions that firms can ask to help identify problems or opportunities that require a change in the current process or system for a change program. By answering these questions, firms can gain a better understanding of the problem that requires a change in the current process and develop a clear plan for addressing it.
Pain points	What are the current pain points or issues within the firm?
Root causes	What are the root causes of these issues?
ASIS processes	What are the current processes and systems in place, and are they effective?
Issues impact	How do these issues affect the organization's overall performance and goals?
Benefits	What are the potential benefits of addressing these issues?
Risks	What are the potential risks of not addressing these issues?
Stakeholders	What are the opinions of key stakeholders, including employees and customers, on these issues?
Industries	What are other organizations in similar industries or with similar processes doing to address similar issues?

1.1 Change need process

General overview	The process to identify a problem or opportunity that requires a change in the current process or system for a change program typically includes the following steps:
Assess ASIS processes	Assess the current processes, systems, and firm's structure to identify areas that are not working effectively or efficiently.
Root cause analysis	Identify the root cause of the problem or opportunity. Determine the underlying reasons for the problem or opportunity, rather than just addressing symptoms.
issue prioritization	Prioritize the issues by ranking the identified problems and opportunities based on their impact and urgency.
Potential solutions	Develop potential solutions to generate a range of potential solutions to address the problem or opportunity.
Selection of best solution	Select the best solution by evaluating the potential solutions and select the one that best addresses the problem while considering the feasibility and potential impact on the firm.
Execution plan for solution	Develop a plan to implement the solution that outlines the steps required to implement the selected solution.
Monitor and evaluate change program	Continuously monitor and evaluate the change program: effectiveness so that it is meeting its objectives.

1.1 Change need process - technology

General overview	The process for identifying an opportunity for technological innovation for a change program can involve several steps:
Identify the problem or opportunity	Understand the problem or opportunity that the change program is trying to address.
Conduct a technology scan	Research and evaluate existing technologies that could potentially solve the problem or take advantage of the opportunity.
Identify gaps	Identify any gaps in current technology that could be filled by developing new technology.
Assess feasibility	Assess the feasibility of developing new technology to fill the identified gaps.
Conceptualize the solution	Develop a conceptual solution that leverages technology to address the problem or opportunity.
Evaluate potential impact	Evaluate the potential impact of the proposed technology solution on the organization and its stakeholders.
Develop a plan	Develop a plan to implement the technology solution as part of the change program.

1.1 Change need - root cause analysis

General overview	Root cause analysis techniques like the 5 Whys, Fishbone diagrams, and Pareto Charts are commonly used to identify and analyse the root cause of a problem. The process steps to identify the root cause of a problem typically are:
Define the problem	Define the problem and understand the scope of the issue.
Collect data	Gather data related to the problem or opportunity, including facts, statistics, and customer feedback.
Identify patterns	Analyse the data and identify patterns and trends that may indicate the root cause of the problem or opportunity.
Develop hypotheses	Develop hypotheses about the possible causes of the problem based on the patterns and trends identified.
Test hypotheses	Test the hypotheses by conducting further research through interviewing experts and observing processes.
Identify the root cause	Use the data and insights gathered to identify the root cause of the problem or opportunity.
Confirm root cause:	Verify the identified root cause through additional testing.
Communicate the root cause	Communicate the root cause of the problem or opportunity to the stakeholders and teams involved in the change program.

=

1.1 Change need best practices

General overview	There are several best practices for identifying the root cause of a problem or opportunity that requires a change in the current process or system for a change program, including:
Involve a diverse group of stakeholders	Gather a team from different departments of the firm to provide different perspectives and insights on the problem.
Use a structured approach	Use a structured approach such as root cause analysis techniques like the 5 Whys, Fishbone diagrams, and Pareto Charts to identify and analyse the root cause of the problem.
Focus on the process, not the people	While it may be tempting to blame individuals for problems, it is important to focus on the process and the systems that may be contributing to the problem or opportunity.
Gather data from multiple sources	Collect data from multiple sources such as customer feedback, process data, and employee observations to get a comprehensive understanding of the problem or opportunity.
Keep an open mind	Be open to new ideas and perspectives, and be willing to consider a wide range of possible causes for the problem.
Verify the root cause	Once a root cause is identified, it's important to verify it through additional testing and analysis.
Communicate the root cause	Communicate the root cause of the problem to the relevant stakeholders involved in the change program. This will help them understand the problem, and be able to address it.
Continuously monitor & evaluate the process	The process of identifying the root cause should not be a one-time effort, but should be continuously monitored, evaluated and improved.

1.1 Change need risks

General overview	There are several risks associated with identifying or not identifying the root cause of a problem that requires a change in the current process or system including:
Inaccurate problem definition	If the problem is not accurately identified, it can lead to a misdiagnosis of the problem and an inappropriate solution.
Ineffective solutions	If the root cause of the problem is not identified, the implemented solution may not address the actual problem.
Wasted resources	Resources may be wasted on implementing solutions that do not address the problem.
Lack of buy-in	It may be difficult to gain buy-in from stakeholders and employees for the change program if root cause not found.
Unintended consequences	Implementing a solution may have unintended consequences that create new problems and still not solve the original one.
Lack of Continuous improvement	The problem may continue to occur and may not be resolved permanently If the root cause is not identified and addressed,
Lack of proper communication	It can lead to misunderstandings and lack of proper communication among the stakeholders.
Difficulty in measuring the effectiveness	Without identifying the root cause, it will be difficult to measure the effectiveness of the implemented solution and continuously improve the process.

1.1 Change need lessons learned

General overview	There are several lessons that can be learned from identifying or not identifying the root cause of a problem that requires a change in the current process or system including:
Importance of accurate problem definition	Identifying the root cause of a problem requires an accurate definition of the problem to find the correct solution.
Structured approach	Using a structured approach as root cause analysis ensures that the root cause of a problem is accurately identified.
Data-driven decision making	Gather data from multiple sources to understand the problem and make data-driven decisions.
Diverse team	A diverse group of stakeholders in the root cause analysis process can provide different perspectives and insights.
Continuous improvement	Continuously monitoring and evaluating the process can lead to identifying new root causes and improve the process.
Effective communication	Identifying the root cause of a problem and communicating it to the r stakeholders can help them understand the problem.
Measuring effectiveness	Measure the effectiveness of the implemented solution and continuously improve the process.
The need for flexibility	Being open to new ideas and perspectives, and being willing to consider a wide range of possible causes for the problem.

1.2 Assess Impact

The purpose of an impact assessment is to evaluate the potential effects of a proposed change program on a particular process or system. The goals of an impact assessment include identifying any potential risks or negative impacts associated with the proposed change, as well as any potential benefits or positive impacts.

Additionally, an impact assessment can help identify any areas of the process or system that may need to be modified or improved in order to optimize the effectiveness of the proposed change program. Overall, the goal of an impact assessment is to ensure that the proposed change program is well-designed and well-executed, and that it will achieve the desired outcomes in a sustainable and efficient manner.

The consequences of conducting an impact assessment that requires a change in the current process or system for a change program can vary depending on the specific circumstances of the proposed change.

Some potential positive consequences of an impact assessment include:

- By identifying potential risks and benefits, an impact assessment can help decision-makers make more informed decisions about whether to proceed with the proposed change program, and how to implement it.
- By involving stakeholders in the impact assessment process, it can increase the likelihood that they will support the change program.
- On the other hand, some potential negative consequences of an impact assessment include:
- Conducting an impact assessment can require significant time and resources, which could delay the execution of the change program.
- By involving stakeholders in the impact assessment process, it may raise awareness and resistance to the change program if they perceive it as having a negative impact on them.

Overall, it is best practices to perform an impact assessment for the benefits it offers towards the success of a change program.

1.2 Assess impact workstream activities

Define change	**Define the change.**
	Clearly outline the scope, objectives, and desired outcomes of the change is the first step in assessing its impact.
Stakeholders	**Identify stakeholders.**
	Understanding who will be affected by the change and how is important for determining the potential impact of the change.
Assess impact	**Assess the impact.**
	Analyse the potential impact of the change on various areas such as costs, benefits, risks, and opportunities.
Change Comms	**Communicate the change,**
	Communicate the change and its potential impact to all stakeholders is important for ensuring that they are prepared for the change and understand its implications.
Monitor	**Monitoring & evaluate change.**
	Continuously monitor the change and evaluate its impact is necessary to ensure that the change achieves its desired objectives and to make any necessary adjustments.
Assess impact target	**Assess the impact.**
	Determine the potential impact of the change on various stakeholders (staff, customers, and the firm as a whole).

1.2 Assess impact questions

General overview	Some key questions for an impact assessment on a proposed change for a change program may include:
Scope & scale	What is the scope and scale of the proposed change?
Impacted stakeholders	Who will be affected by the change, and how?
Change consequences	What are the positive & negative impacts of the change?
Firm performance	How will the change impact firm performance and outcomes?
Staff roles & responsibilities	How will the change impact employees, including their roles, responsibilities, and skills?
Customer impacts	How will the change impact customers or other stakeholders?
Change comms	How change be communicated to affected parties?
Resource requirements	What resources (financial, personnel, technology) will be required to implement the change?
Risk management	What are the risks associated with the change, and how will they be mitigated?
Success measures	How will the success of the change be measured and evaluated?

1.2 Assess impact process

General overview	The process steps for an impact assessment on a proposed change for a change program may include:
The scope and goals of the impact assessment	Identify the proposed change and its goals & specific areas and stakeholders that will be affected by the change.
Identify and assess the impact of the change	Analyse the positive and negative impacts of the change on various areas (firm performance, staff, customers)
Identify and evaluate the resources required	Determine the resources, including financial, personnel, and technology, needed to implement the change.
Identify and assess the risks	Identify the risks with the change, including the likelihood of each risk occurring and the potential impact if it does.
Develop a plan for mitigating risks	Develop a plan for mitigating or managing the risks identified and the actions that will be taken to minimize them.
Develop a communication plan	Develop a comms plan for how the change will be communicated to staff, customers, and other stakeholders.
Develop a monitoring and evaluation plan	Develop a plan for how the change will be monitored and evaluated and KPIs & metrics to measure change success.
Execute the plan	Execute the change program, the mitigation & comms plans.
Monitor and evaluate	Continuously monitor and evaluate the change program using the metrics and KPIs & make adjustments as needed.
Communicate the results	Communicate the results of the impact assessment and any follow-up actions to all relevant stakeholders.

1.2 Assess impact on processes & systems

General overview	Some key questions for an impact assessment on a proposed change to a process or system for a change:
Owners	Who is the process or system owner?
Impacted stakeholders	Who are the impacted stakeholders?
Name & operation	What is the current process or system and how does it work?
Proposed change	What is the proposed change to the process or system>
Improvement	How will the change improve the process or system?
Potential impacts on process or system	What are the potential positive and negative impacts of the proposed change on process efficiency and effectiveness?
The impact on stakeholders	How will the proposed change impact the stakeholders (staff, customers, suppliers, etc.) involved in the process or system?
Impact risks	What are the risks associated with the proposed change?
Change comms	How will the change be communicated to stakeholders?
Resources required	What resources will be required to implement the change?
Success metrics	How will the success of the change be measured?
Long terms effects	What are the potential long-term effects of the change?

1.2 Assess impact - process mapping

General overview	The process map session is a technique used to understand, document and analyse the current process, and it can help to identify inefficiencies, bottlenecks, and opportunities for improvement. This data can then be used to develop a new process that is more efficient, effective, and aligned with the goals and objectives of the change program. This information can also be used as a base for creating a detailed implementation plan and a monitoring plan to evaluate the success of the new process. The key steps for conducting a process map workshop session are the following but the specifics steps may vary depending on the organization, the process and the program.
Process owner	Identify the owner of the process.
Define the scope of the process	Identify the specific process or processes that will be mapped, and define the boundaries of the process in terms of inputs, outputs, and key stakeholders.
Assemble the team	Assemble a team who are familiar with the process and who will be involved in the process mapping workshop.
Prepare a process map template	Prepare a process map template to be used to document the process. This template will include all the necessary elements (process steps, inputs, outputs, and decision points).

1.2 Assess impact - process mapping

Conduct the workshop	Conduct the workshop with the team members who will be involved in the process mapping. This typically involves walking through the process step by step and documenting it on the process map template.
Analyse the process	Once the process is documented, analyse it to identify inefficiencies, bottlenecks & opportunities for improvement.
Identify and prioritize improvements	Identify and prioritize the improvements that will be made as part of the change program.
Review and validate the process map	Review the process map with stakeholders to ensure that it is accurate and complete, and to validate the improvements.
Create a detailed implementation plan and monitoring plan	Create a detailed implementation plan that outlines the specific tasks, activities, and timelines required to implement the improvements. Also create a monitoring plan to evaluate the success of the new process.

1.2 Process mapping best practices

Scopes & objectives of mapping session	Clearly defining the scope and objectives of the process mapping session.
Involving key stakeholders	Identifying and involving key stakeholders who have a deep understanding of the process being mapped.
Using standardized process mapping	Using a standardized process mapping notation, such as BPMN or Flowchart, to ensure consistency and clarity.
Verify accuracy of process map	Verifying the accuracy of the process map through testing and validation with process owners and users.
Continuously review & updating process map	Continuously reviewing and updating the process map as the change program progresses to ensure it remains accurate.
Communicating the process map	Communicating the process map to all relevant parties and making it easily accessible for reference and training.
Incorporating feedback	Incorporating customer and employee feedback to identify areas for improvement and optimize the process.

1.2 Assess impact best practices

Involve key stakeholders in the assessment process	Involve key stakeholders (staff, customers, and other impacted parties, in the impact assessment process so that their perspectives and concerns are taken into account.
Use a structured approach	Use a structured approach to the impact assessment (a checklist) so that all areas are considered and evaluated.
Short-term and long-term impacts	Consider the short-term and long-term impacts of the change on different areas and stakeholders.
Be transparent in communications	Communicate the results of the impact assessment to all relevant stakeholders and be transparent about the impacts.
Continuously monitor and evaluate	Continuously monitor and evaluate the change program to ensure that it is meeting its intended goals.
Use a multi-disciplinary approach	Use a multi-disciplinary approach that includes experts from different areas of the firm, such as IT, HR, and finance.
Assess the impact on the customer	Assess the impact of the change on the customer experience & how it will affect customer service and satisfaction.
Assess the impact on the employees	Assess the impact of the change on the staff and how it will affect their roles, responsibilities, and overall engagement.
Be flexible and adaptable	Be flexible and adaptable, and be prepared to make adjustments so that the change program is successful.

1.2 Assess impact risks

General overview	Some risks that may be considered during an impact assessment on a proposed change to a process or system for a change program include:
Operational risks	May disrupt existing operations and cause delays, errors, or other issues that can impact efficiency and effectiveness.
Financial risks	The proposed change may be too expensive, not generate the expected cost savings or not deliver revenue increases.
Technical risks	New technology or systems risks when they are untested or unproven, leading to technical problems or failures.
Human resource risks	Employees roles, responsibilities, or skills may be impacted leading to resistance, low morale, or a high rate of turnover.
Security risks	Changes may increase the risk of data breaches, cyber-attacks, or other security incidents.
Reputation risks	Some changes can negatively impact the company's reputation with customers, suppliers, or other stakeholders.
Dependency risks	The change may rely on other processes or systems that are not fully in place, or may negatively impact other systems.
Integration risks	There could be integration issues with existing processes or systems, leading to incompatibility problems.
Implementation risks	The change may be difficult to implement, or may not be implemented as planned, leading to delays or other issues.

1.2 Assess impact lessons learned

General overview	Some lessons that can be learned from an impact assessment for a change program include:
Involve stakeholders in the assessment	Involve key stakeholders in the impact assessment process co that their perspectives and concerns are taken into account, and can increase buy-in and support for the change.
Consider short-term and long-term impacts	Consider both short-term and long-term impacts of the proposed change on different areas and stakeholders, including the potential for unintended consequences.
Effective communications	Effective communication is critical so that the proposed change is understood and supported by all stakeholders.
Monitor and evaluate change program	Continuous monitoring and evaluation of the program so that it meets its goals and that any issues or risks are addressed.
Be flexible and adaptability	Change programs are more likely to be successful if they are flexible and adaptable, and if they adjust as needed.
Conduct a risk assessment	Conduct a comprehensive risk assessment to identify and mitigate risks associated with the proposed change.
Consider the impact on the customer	Consider the impact of the change on the customer experience, including how it will affect customer service, product or service quality, and overall satisfaction.
Consider the impact on the employees	Consider the impact of the change on the staff and how it will affect their roles, responsibilities, and overall engagement.
Have a clear execution plan	A clear execution plan is crucial so that the change is implemented as planned, and that the change is successful.

1.3 Change goals

The purpose of setting goals and objectives for a change program is to clearly define the desired outcome of the change and to provide a roadmap for achieving it. Goals and objectives help to focus the efforts of the change team, align stakeholders around a common vision, and measure progress towards the desired outcome. They also provide a way to evaluate the effectiveness of the change program and make adjustments as needed.

SMART goals and objectives are specific, measurable, attainable, relevant, and time-bound. Here are a few examples of SMART goals and objectives for a change program:

Example

- **Specific:** Increase employee engagement by 20% within the next 12 months.

- **Measurable:** Implement a survey to measure employee engagement and track progress towards the goal.

- **Attainable:** Develop a comprehensive training program for managers on how to effectively engage employees.

- **Relevant:** Employee engagement is a key driver of productivity and turnover, so good engagement is important for the success of the firm

- **Time-bound:** Achieve the goal of increasing employee engagement by the end of the next fiscal year.

Poorly defined change goals and objectives can make it difficult for the organization to achieve its desired outcomes and can impede the success of the change program.

Without clear goals and objectives, it may be difficult for stakeholders to understand the purpose of the change program and how it aligns with the overall goals of the organization. This can lead to confusion and lack of buy-in from key stakeholders.

1.3 Change goals workstream activities

Business need	**Identify the business need.**
	Understand the problem that the change is intended to address, and align it with the goals and strategy of the firm.
Stakeholders	**Engage key stakeholders.**
	Engage key stakeholders in the change process for their buy-in and support by identifying who will be affected by the change and gathering their input and feedback.
Change goals	**Define clear objectives.**
	Establish specific, measurable, achievable, relevant, and time-bound (SMART) objectives for the change that can be used to track progress and measure success.
Priorities	**Prioritize and plan.**
	Prioritize the objectives and develop a plan to achieve them, identifying the resources, timelines, and responsibilities.
Comms & align	**Communicate and align objectives.**
	Communicate the objectives and plan to all stakeholders, and so they are aligned with the goals and strategy of the firm. Regularly review progress and adjust the plan as needed.
Define Goals	**Define change objectives.**
	Define objectives involves establishing clear and measurable objectives for the change program.

1.3 Change goals questions

General overview	There are several key questions that firms should consider when setting goals and objectives for a change program. Overall, these questions are important so that the goals and objectives of the change program are clear, aligned with the firm's goals & achievable within the given resources and time.
Desired outcome of the change	**What is the desired outcome of the change program?**
	This question helps to define the overall goal of the program, so that all stakeholders are aligned on the desired outcome.
Impacted stakeholders by the change	**Who will be affected by the change program?**
	Understand the stakeholders who will be impacted by the change program is important to identify potential resistance and address any concerns they may have.
Objectives and goals to be achieved	**What are the objectives that need to be achieved?**
	Define specific, measurable objectives helps to break down the overall goal into steps and allows to track progress.
Resources required to achieve goals	**What resources will be required to achieve the goals?**
	Identify the resources needed to implement the program so the firm has the resources to support the change effort.
Success metrics	**How will success be measured?**
	Define how success to be measured for tracking progress to determine the overall success of the change program.
Sustainability actions	**How will the changes be sustained?**
	The change program should not only focus on the implementation of the change but also on the maintenance and continuity of the change.

1.3 Change goals process

General overview	he process for creating change goals and objectives for a change program typically includes the following steps:
Identify the need for change	Identify the problem that is driving the need for change as a decrease in productivity or customer satisfaction.
Define the goal of the change program	Define the overall goal of the change program (specific, measurable, and aligned with the firm's overall goals.
Identify stakeholders	Understand who will be affected by the change program is and identify potential resistance and address any issues.
Develop specific objectives	To achieve the overall goal, specific objectives need to be developed. These objectives should SMART.
Assess the resources required	Identify the resources needed to implement the change program so the firm has the resources to support the change.
Develop a plan of action	Develop a plan of action that outlines the specific steps that need to be taken to achieve the objectives and goal.
Communicate the plan	Communicate the plan to all stakeholders (employees, leaders and any parties impacted by the change program.
Monitor progress	Monitoring progress so that the change program is on track and making progress towards achieving the objectives.
Evaluate and adjust	As the change program progresses, it is important to evaluate its effectiveness and make adjustments as needed.
Sustain the change	Take action so that the changes are sustained over time and that they continue to bring value to the organization.

1.3 Change goals best practices

General overview	By following these best practices, firms can ensure that their change goals and objectives are clear, aligned with the firm's overall goals, and achievable within the given resources. This will increase the chances of success of the change program.
Keep it simple and specific	Goals and objectives should be clear, concise, and easy to understand and be specific and focus on a single outcome.
Make them measurable	Goals and objectives should be measurable so that progress can be tracked and success can be determined.
Align with the firm's overall goals	Goals and objectives should align with the firm's overall goals and strategy to ensure that they support the firm's and vision.
Involve stakeholders	Involve key stakeholders in the process of setting goals and objectives so that the goals and objectives are aligned with the needs and concerns of those who will be impacted.
Set realistic and achievable goals	Goals and objectives should be realistic and achievable within the given timeframe and with the available resources.
Prioritize	Prioritize the goals so the most important ones are done first.
Communicate	Communicate the goals and objectives to all stakeholders to ensure that everyone is aware of what needs to be achieved.
Review and adjust	Review and adjust the goals so they are still relevant.
Sustainability	Ensure the goals and objectives are sustainable over time.
Prepare for contingencies	Make plans for contingencies, unexpected events and obstacles that could impede the change program.

1.3 Change goals risks

General overview	There are several risks associated with creating change goals and objectives for a change program. By recognizing and managing these risks, firm can ensure that their change goals and objectives are clear, aligned, achievable and sustainable and this increase the chances of success.
Unrealistic goals	Setting unrealistic goals and objectives can lead to disappointment and demotivation among stakeholders and can ultimately hinder the success of the change program.
Lack of buy-in	If goals are not clearly communicated or if stakeholders are not involved in the process of setting them, it can lead to a lack of buy-in and commitment to the change program.
Misaligned goals	Goals and objectives that are not aligned with the organization's overall goals and strategy can lead to confusion and inefficiency, and can ultimately hinder the success of the change program.

1.3 Change goals risks

Resistance to change	If goals and objectives are not clearly communicated or if stakeholders are not involved in the process of setting them, it can lead to resistance to change among stakeholders.
Lack of flexibility	If goals and objectives are set without considering potential changes in the environment, it can make it difficult to adjust and adapt as needed, leading to a lack of flexibility.
Limited Resources	If the goals are not aligned with the resources available, it can lead to an inability to achieve the desired outcome.
Overcomplication	Setting too many goals and objectives can be overwhelming, and can lead to confusion among stakeholders and a lack of focus on what's important.
Short-sightedness	Setting goals that only address short-term needs, rather than long-term sustainability, can lead to future problems.

1.3 Change goals lessons learned

General overview	Creating change goals and objectives for a change program can be a complex process, and there are several lessons that organizations can learn from past experiences.
Involve stakeholders early	Involving key stakeholders in the process of setting goals ensures that the goals are aligned with the needs and concerns of those impacted by the change program.
Keep it simple and specific	Goals should be clear, concise, and easy to understand. They should be specific and focus on a single outcome.
Align with the firm's overall goals	Goals and objectives should align with the firm's overall goals and strategy so that they support the firm's vision.
Communicate effectively	Communicate the goals and objectives to all stakeholders so that everyone is aware of what needs to be achieved and how they can support the change program.
Monitor progress	Regularly monitor progress so that the change program is on track and making progress towards achieving the objectives.
Be prepared for resistance	Resistance to change is a common occurrence, and organizations should be prepared to address it effectively.
Flexibility and adaptability	Be prepared to adjust and adapt as needed in order to ensure that the goals are still relevant and achievable.
Sustainability	Ensure that the goals are sustainable over time and that they will continue to bring value to the organization.
Continuous improvement	Continuously evaluate the change program and adjust as needed to improve its effectiveness over time.

1.4 Change Plan

The purpose of a strategic organization change management program is to effectively plan, implement and manage changes within an organization to achieve specific goals and objectives.

These goals and objectives may include:

- Improving overall organizational performance
- Increasing efficiency and productivity
- Enhancing customer satisfaction
- Improving employee engagement and morale
- Aligning the organization with its mission and vision
- Adapting to changes in the business environment
- Implementing new technology or processes
- Reducing costs
- Increasing revenue
- Improving the organization's competitive position

The goal of a strategic organization change management program is to ensure that changes are implemented smoothly, effectively, and with minimal disruption to the organization and its employees, and stakeholders.

Not having a plan for a strategic organization change management program can have a number of negative impacts on an organization, including:

Without a plan, changes can disrupt the delivery of products or services to customers, leading to damage to customer relationships and potentially lost business.

The changes may not align with the organization's overall goals and objectives, which can lead to wasted resources and a lack of progress towards those goals. Also, it can be difficult to measure the success of changes, making it hard to determine if they are achieving the desired goals.

1.4 Change plan activities

Define change	**Define the change.**
	Clearly identify the scope and objectives of the change, as well as the stakeholders involved.
Assess impact	**Assess the change impact.**
	Understand the potential impact of the change on the organization, including any risks or challenges that may arise.
Change plan	**Develop a detailed change plan.**
	Create a detailed plan outlining the steps to implement the change, including timelines, resources, and milestones.
Comms Plan	**Communicate the change plan.**
	Communicate the change plan to all relevant stakeholders, including employees, managers, and other key parties.
Execution	**Execute the change plan.**
	Execute the change plan, monitor progress, and adjust as needed so the change is implemented successfully.
Change plan outcome	**Develop a detailed plan.**
	Create a detailed plan for implementing the change, including tasks, timelines, and resource requirements.

1.4 Change plan questions

General overview	Answering these questions would be a good starting point to develop a comprehensive change plan.
ASIS state	What is the current state of the firm?
Goals & objectives	What are the goals & objectives of the change program?
Impacted stakeholders	Who are the stakeholders impacted by the change program?
Potential barriers	What are the potential barriers to a successful change?
Resources required	What resources (financial, personnel, technical, etc.) will be needed to implement the change program?
Tasks & activities	What are the specific tasks and activities that will need to be completed to implement the change program?
Task responsibility	Who will be responsible for doing each task and activity?
Risk management	What are the risks associated with the change program and how will they be managed?
Change progress	How will progress towards the goals and objectives of the change program be measured and reported?
Sustainability	How will the change program be sustained after execution?

1.4 Change plan process

General overview	The process steps to develop a change plan for a change program can vary depending on firm and change program,
Define the problem or opportunity	Clearly define the problem or opportunity that the change program is trying to address.
Assess the current state	Assess the current state of the firm (processes, systems, and culture, in order to understand how they may be impacted.
Identify the desired state	Identify the desired state that the organization should achieve after the change program has been implemented.
Identify the key stakeholders	Identify the stakeholders that will be impacted by the change program (employees, customers, and other relevant parties).
Conduct a gap analysis	Conduct a gap analysis to identify the differences between the current state and the desired state, and to determine what actions need to be taken to bridge that gap.
Develop a strategy	Develop a strategy for implementing the change program, including specific goals, objectives, and action plans.

1.4 Change plan process

Identify and plan for resistance	Identify potential sources of resistance to the change program and develop a plan to address them.
Build a cross-functional team	Build a cross functional team to manage the change program, including assigning roles and responsibilities.
Develop a communication plan	Develop a communication plan to keep stakeholders informed and engaged throughout the change program.
Identify and plan for contingencies	Identify potential risks and obstacles that could impact the change program and develop a plan to address them.
Implement and monitor the change	Implement the change program, monitoring progress and making adjustments as necessary.
Sustain the change	Once the change program is implemented, develop a plan to sustain the change over the long-term, including monitoring progress and making adjustments as necessary.

1.4 Change plan components

General overview	A change plan for a change program typically includes the following components:
Problem statement or opportunity	A clear and concise statement of the problem or opportunity that the change program is trying to address.
Goals and objectives	Specific, measurable, and time-bound goals and objectives that the change program is trying to achieve.
Stakeholder analysis	Identification and analysis of key stakeholders that will be impacted by the change program(their roles, needs, and potential resistance).
Current state analysis:	An assessment of the ASIS of the organization, including its processes, systems, and culture, in order to understand how they may be impacted by the change program.
Desired state	A clear and detailed description of the desired state that the firm will achieve after the change program is executed
Gap analysis	Identification of the differences between the current state and the desired state, and determination of what actions need to be taken to bridge that gap.

1.4 Change plan components

Change strategy	A detailed plan for implementing the change program, including specific goals, objectives, and action plans.
Implementation plan	A detailed plan that outlines the specific tasks, activities, and timelines required to implement the change program.
Resource plan	Identification of the resources (financial, personnel, technical, etc.) that will be required to implement the change program.
Communication plan	A plan for communicating with stakeholders throughout the change program (the methods and frequency of comms).
Risk management plan	Identification and assessment of potential risks of the change program, and a plan for mitigating or managing those risks.
Monitoring and evaluation plan	A plan for monitoring progress towards the goals and objectives of the change program, and for evaluating the effectiveness of the change program.
Sustainability plan	A plan for maintaining and sustaining the changes made by the change program after it has been implemented.

1.4 Change plan best practices

General overview	Here are some best practices for developing a change plan for a change program.
Start with a clear problem statement or opportunity	Clearly define the problem or opportunity that the change program is trying to address. This will provide a clear focus for the change plan and help to ensure that the goals and objectives of the change program are aligned with the organization's overall strategy.
Involve key stakeholders in the planning process	Involve key stakeholders (staff, customers, and other relevant parties), in the planning process so that their needs and concerns are taken into account and that the change program is more likely to be accepted and implemented successfully.
Conduct a thorough current state analysis	Conduct a thorough analysis of the current state of the organization, including its processes, systems, and culture. This will provide a solid foundation for identifying the desired state and the gap that needs to be bridged.
Identify SMART goals and objectives	Identify specific, measurable, and time-bound goals and objectives for the change program so that the change program is focused and that progress is tracked & reported.
Develop a detailed change strategy	Develop a comprehensive change strategy that addresses all aspects of the change program, including goals and objectives, key activities, timelines, and resource needs.

1.4 Change plan best practices

Develop a detailed implementation plan	Develop a detailed implementation plan that outlines the specific tasks, activities, and timelines required to implement the change program.
Identify and plan for potential resistance	Identify potential sources of resistance to the change program and develop a plan to address them. This will help to minimize disruptions and ensure a smooth implementation.
Develop a comms plan	Develop a communication plan that keeps stakeholders informed and engaged throughout the change program.
Identify and plan for contingencies	Identify potential risks and obstacles that could impact the change program and develop a plan to address them.
Monitor and evaluate progress	Monitor progress towards the goals and objectives of the change program, and evaluate the effectiveness of the change program. This will help to identify areas where adjustments are needed and to ensure that the change program is achieving its intended results.
Sustain the change	Once the change program is implemented, develop a plan to sustain the change over the long-term, including monitoring progress and making adjustments as necessary.

1.4 Change plan risks

General overview	Developing a change plan for a change program can come with several risks. To mitigate these risks, it is important to have a clear problem statement, involving key stakeholders, conducting thorough analysis, setting specific, measurable and time-bound goals, having a comprehensive change strategy, having a detailed implementation plan, having a communication plan, having a monitoring and evaluation plan, having a risk management plan and having a sustainability plan in the change plan.
Misaligned goals	If the goals and objectives of the change plan are not aligned with the overall strategy of the organization, it can lead to confusion and resistance among stakeholders.
Inadequate resources	If the change plan is not adequately resourced, it can lead to delays or the plan being implemented poorly.
Lack of buy-in	If key stakeholders are not involved in the planning process, or if their concerns and needs are not adequately addressed in the change plan, it can lead to lack of buy-in and resistance to the change program.

1.4 Change plan risks

Unforeseen obstacles	There may be unforeseen obstacles or risks that arise during the change program, which can impact the timeline and success of the change plan.
Inadequate communication	If the comms plan is not well-designed, it can lead to confusion, lack of buy-in, &resistance among stakeholders.
Difficulty in measuring the progress	If the progress and results of the change program are not easily measurable, it can be difficult to evaluate the effectiveness of the change plan and adjust as needed.
Lack of sustainability	If the change plan does not have a sustainability plan, it can lead to the changes being undone after program is over.

1.4 Change plan lessons learned

General overview	Developing a change plan for a change program can be a complex process, and there can be many lessons learned.
Clearly define the problem or opportunity	It is important to start with a clear and concise statement of the problem or opportunity that the change program is trying to address. This will provide a clear focus for the change plan and help to ensure that the goals and objectives of the change program are aligned with the firm's overall strategy.
Involve key stakeholders early	Involving key stakeholders, including employees, customers, and other relevant parties, early in the planning process can help to ensure that their needs and concerns are taken into account and that the change program is more likely to be accepted and implemented successfully.
Conduct a thorough current state analysis	Conducting a thorough analysis of the current state of the organization, including its processes, systems, and culture, can provide a solid foundation for identifying the desired state and the gap that needs to be bridged.
Be realistic about timelines	Change plans often require more time and resources than initially anticipated. It's important to be realistic about timelines and to build in contingencies for delays.
Communicate effectively	Developing a clear and effective communication plan is essential to the success of the change program. It helps to keep stakeholders informed and engaged, and can help to build buy-in and support for the change program.
Be prepared for resistance	Resistance to change is a common occurrence, and it's key to be prepared for it and to have a plan in place to address it.

1.5 Comms

The purposes, objectives and goals for communications as part of the assessment phase of a change program include:

- Informing stakeholders about the change program, including the reasons for the change, the goals and objectives of the program, and how it will impact them.
- Gathering input and feedback from stakeholders to help shape the design and execution of the program.
- Building buy-in and support for the change program by communicating its benefits and addressing any concerns or resistance.
- Ensuring that all stakeholders have a clear understanding of their roles and responsibilities in the program.
- Keeping stakeholders informed of progress and any changes to the program as it progresses.

- Communicating the results of the assessment phase, including any identified issues for improvement.
- Creating a sense of shared ownership and collaboration among stakeholders to increase the chances of success for the change program.

Not having communications as part of the assessment phase of a change program can have a number of negative impacts, including:

- Lack of buy-in and support from stakeholders, who may be resistant to or unaware of the change program.
- Misunderstandings and confusion about the purpose, goals and objectives of the change program among stakeholders.
- Difficulty in identifying and addressing resistance from stakeholders.
- Limited input and feedback from stakeholders, which can result in a poorly implemented program.
- Poor communication can also lead to negative impact on customer and employees, leading to further issues.

1.5 Comms activities

Stakeholders	Identify stakeholders.
	Understand who the stakeholders are and what their specific concerns and interests are related to the change.
Comms plan	Develop a comms plan.
	Create a comms plan that outlines key messages, channels, and timing to communicate the change to stakeholders.
Regular comms	Communicate regularly.
	Keep stakeholders informed of progress, changes, and any issues that arise throughout the change process.
Feedback	Listen & respond to feedback.
	Encourage stakeholders to provide feedback, and listen and respond to any concerns or questions they may have.
Channels	Use different comms channels.
	Use a variety of communication channels, such as email, meetings, and video conferencing, to reach different stakeholders and ensure the message is received by all.
Comms outcome	Communicate the change plan.
	Communicate effectively the change program to stakeholders to gain their buy-in and support for the plan.

1.5 Comms questions

General overview	These questions can help guide the communication strategy and ensure that all stakeholders are informed, engaged and on board with the change program. The key questions for communications as part of the assessment phase are:
Key stakeholders	Who are the key stakeholders that need to be informed and engaged during the assessment phase?
Message to be communicated	What is the message that needs to be communicated to stakeholders about the change program?
The impacts on stakeholders	How will the change program impact different stakeholders and what are their specific concerns?
Stakeholders informed and engaged	How will stakeholders be informed and engaged during the assessment phase?
Feedback process and its use for inputs	How will feedback and input from stakeholders be gathered and used in the design and execution of the program?
Progress status communications	How will progress and changes to the program be communicated to stakeholders?
Stakeholder roles & responsibilities	How will stakeholders be made aware of their roles and responsibilities in the change program?
Assessment success measures	How will we measure the success of the communications during the assessment phase?
Resistance plan	How will we handle resistance raised by stakeholders?
Comms timeliness and quality	How will we ensure that communication is timely, accurate and consistent throughout the assessment phase?

1.5 Comms process

General overview	The process steps for creating communications as part of the assessment phase of a change program include:
Identify key stakeholders	Determine who needs to be informed and engaged during the assessment phase and what their specific concerns may be.
Develop a comms plan	Define the message that needs to be communicated to stakeholders, the channels and timing that will be used.
Prepare comms materials	Create materials such as presentations, brochures, and FAQs that will be used to inform and engage stakeholders.
Conduct stakeholder engagement	Communicate with stakeholders through different channels such as meetings, webinars, newsletters and email updates.
Gather feedback and input	Encourage stakeholders to provide feedback and input on the change program, and incorporate this feedback into it. design
Communicate progress and changes	Keep stakeholders informed of progress and any changes to the program, and address any concerns that may arise.
Assign roles and responsibilities	Communicate stakeholders' roles and responsibilities in the change program & provide training and support as needed.
Measure success	Evaluate the effectiveness of the communications and make adjustments as needed.
Continuously review and improve	Continuously review the comms plan and approach, and make improvements as necessary so that stakeholders are well informed & engaged throughout the assessment phase.

1.5 Comms plan components

General overview	A well-designed and executed communications plan will help ensure that stakeholders are informed & engaged, and on board with the change program. The components for creating a comms plan as part of the assessment phase are:
Objectives and goals	Clearly define the objectives and goals for the comms plan, and the desired outcomes of the comms.
Audience and stakeholders	Identify the key stakeholders who need to be informed and engaged during the assessment phase, and tailor the comms plan to meet their specific needs and concerns.
Channels of communication	Determine the best channels to use for communicating with stakeholders (meetings, webinars, newsletters, email)
Timing and frequency	Plan the timing and frequency of the comms so that stakeholders are well-informed and engaged.
Key messages	Develop key messages that will be communicated to stakeholders so that they are consistent, clear, and relevant.
Materials and resources	Create materials and resources (presentations, brochures, and FAQs) that will be used to inform & engage stakeholders.
Feedback and input	Plan for how feedback and input from stakeholders will be gathered and use in the execution of the program.
Roles and responsibilities	Assign roles and responsibilities for communicating with stakeholders, and provide training and support as needed.
Evaluation and measurement	Establish a way to evaluate the effectiveness of the communications plan and make adjustments as needed.

1.5 Comms best practices

General overview	During the assessment phase of a change management program, effective communication is crucial in order to gather the necessary information and gain buy-in from stakeholders, and ensure that the change is implemented successfully.
Clearly defining the change	Clearly communicate the purpose, goals and objectives of the proposed change to all stakeholders.
Involving stakeholders	Involve stakeholders in the assessment process, gather their inputs and feedbacks.
Identifying stakeholders	Identify all stakeholders and their level of interest and influence in the change & tailor communication accordingly.
Creating transparency	Create transparency by sharing information about the change and its potential impact on the firm and its stakeholders.
Encouraging open communication	Encourage open communication, actively listen to feedback and respond to questions and concerns.
Update of progress	Keep stakeholders informed of progress & any plan changes.
Regular updates	Provide regular updates on the status of the assessment .
Being responsive	Be responsive to stakeholder's questions and concerns/
Communicating the benefits	Communicate the benefits of the change to all stakeholders, highlighting how it will positively impact the firm & them.
Build trust	Build trust with stakeholders by being honest & transparent.

1.5 Comms risks

General overview	There are several risks associated with communications as part of the assessment phase of a change program. It's important to anticipate these risks, and to have a plan in place to mitigate them. Regularly monitoring and evaluating the communication plan and approach will also help to identify potential risks and make adjustments accordingly.
Inadequate or poor communication	If the communications plan is not well-designed or executed, stakeholders may not be fully informed or engaged, which can lead to resistance and mistrust.
Miscommunication	Miscommunication can lead to confusion, misunderstandings and lack of buy-in from stakeholders can impact the program.
Insufficient feedback and input	If stakeholders don't feel that their feedback is being considered, they may not support the change program.
Resistance and opposition	If stakeholders are not well-informed or engaged, they may be more likely to resist or oppose the change program.
Negative impact on customers and staff	Poor communication can lead to negative impact on customers and employees, leading to further issues.
Delays	Poor comms can lead to delays in execution of the change program as issues are not addressed in a timely manner.
Loss of credibility	If the comms are not timely, accurate, and consistent, it can lead to loss of credibility among stakeholders.

1.5 Comms lessons learned

General overview	Capturing t lessons learned will help to improve the communication plan and approach for future change initiatives. Lessons learned from communications as part of the assessment phase of a change program can include:
Key stakeholders involvement	The importance of involving key stakeholders early on and gathering their feedback and input for buy-in and support.
Clear & consistent messaging	The need for clear and consistent messaging to ensure that stakeholders have a clear understanding of the change program and its goals and objectives.
Use multiple comms channels	The value of using multiple channels of comms to reach different stakeholders so that the message is received by all.
Regular comms	The importance of regularly communicating progress to the program to keep stakeholders informed and engaged.
Effective management of resistance	The need for effective management of resistance and opposition to the change program through clear comms.
Involve people in comms process	The importance of involving customers and employees in the communication process and ensuring their needs are met.
Continuously monitoring	Continuously monitoring and evaluating the comms plan and approach to identify areas for improvement.
The benefits of a comms plan	The benefits of having a comms plan for increased buy-in, better understanding of the change program and its goals.

TO BE IS TO DO.

Immanuel Kant

2.0 Planning

The primary goal of the planning phase in a change management program is to develop a detailed plan for implementing the changes identified during the assessment phase. This includes defining the objectives of the change program, identifying the tasks and resources needed to implement the changes, and developing a schedule for implementing the changes. The planning phase also includes identifying potential risks and developing strategies to mitigate them, as well as creating a communication plan for keeping stakeholders informed about the progress of the change program. The goal of this phase is to have a clear and actionable plan for implementing the changes in the organization.

The 5 key components and associated activities for the planning phase for a change management program?

- Clearly define the scope and goals of the change program and create a shared vision of what will be different as a result of the change.

- Identify all the individuals, groups, and teams who will be affected by the change and determine their level of influence and interest.

- Assess the current readiness of the organization and stakeholders to undertake the change by identifying any potential resistance.

- Create a plan for communicating and engaging with stakeholders throughout the change process.

- Establish a governance structure to oversee the change program, including roles, responsibilities, and decision-making processes.

2.0 Planning Linkages

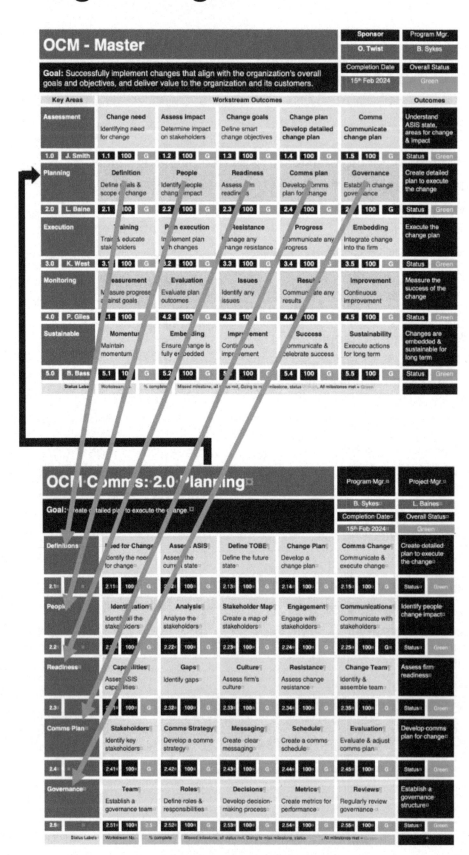

2.0 Planning Workstream Plan

OCM Comms: 2.0 Planning					Program Mgr.	Project Mgr.
Goal: Create detailed plan to execute the change.					B. Sykes	L. Baines
					Completion Date	Overall Status
					15th Feb 2024	Green

Definitions	**Need for Change** Identify the need for change	**Assess ASIS** Assess the current state	**Define TOBE** Define the future state	**Change Plan** Develop a change plan	**Comms Change** Communicate & execute change	Create detailed plan to execute the change
2.1	2.11 100 G	2.12 100 G	2.13 100 G	2.14 100 G	2.15 100 G	Status Green
People	**Identification** Identify all the stakeholders	**Analysis** Analyse the stakeholders	**Stakeholder Map** Create a map of stakeholders	**Engagement** Engage with stakeholders	**Communications** Communicate with stakeholders	Identify people change impact
2.2	2.21 100 G	2.22 100 G	2.23 100 G	2.24 100 G	2.25 100 G	Status Green
Readiness	**Capabilities** Asses ASIS capabilities	**Gaps** Identify gaps	**Culture** Assess firm's culture	**Resistance** Assess change resistance	**Change Team** Identify & assemble team	Assess firm readiness
2.3	2.31 100 G	2.32 100 G	2.33 100 G	2.34 100 G	2.35 100 G	Status Green
Comms Plan	**Stakeholders** Identify key stakeholders	**Comms Strategy** Develop a comms strategy	**Messaging** Create clear messaging	**Schedule** Create a comms schedule	**Evaluation** Evaluate & adjust comms plan	Develop comms plan for change
2.4	2.41 100 G	2.42 100 G	2.43 100 G	2.44 100 G	2.45 100 G	Status Green
Governance	**Team** Establish a governance team	**Roles** Define roles & responsibilities	**Decisions** Develop decision-making process	**Metrics** Create metrics for performance	**Reviews** Regularly review governance	Establish a governance structure
2.5	2.51 100 2.5	2.52 100 G	2.53 100 G	2.54 100 G	2.55 100 G	Status Green

Status Labels	Workstream No.	% complete	Missed milestone, all status red, Going to miss milestone, status , All milestones met = Green

2.1 Definition

The purpose of creating a definition as part of the planning phase for a change program is to establish a clear and shared understanding of the change that is proposed. This definition should include the scope of the change, the desired outcomes, and any relevant constraints or limitations. The goals and objectives of the definition are to:

- Communicate the change to stakeholders and gain their buy-in.
- Identify potential issues or challenges that may arise during the change process.
- Establish a clear and measurable plan for achieving the desired outcomes of the change.
- Provide a basis for monitoring and evaluating the progress and success of the change program.
- Provide a clear and measurable plan for achieving the desired outcomes of the change.

If a definition is not created as part of the planning phase for a change program, it can lead to a number of negative impacts, Without a clear definition:

- Stakeholders may have different understandings of the change and what it entails, leading to confusion and miscommunication.
- Stakeholders may be less likely to support the change, leading to resistance and lack of buy-in.
- Identifying potential issues difficult that may arise during the change process and to develop a plan for addressing them.
- Difficult to monitor and evaluate the progress & success of the program.
- More difficult to know if the desired outcome has been achieved.
- The change process may be delayed due to the need for additional clarification and planning.
- The cost of the change may be higher due to the need for more planning, clarification, and confusion.

2.1 Definition workstream activities

Need for change	Identifying the need for change.
	Identify the problem that requires a change and defining the specific objectives that the change is intended to achieve.
Assess ASIS	Assess the current state.
	Analyse the current situation and identifying the gaps between the current state and the desired state.
Define TOBE	Define the future state.
	Create a detailed description of the desired state that the change is intended to achieve
Change Plan	Develop a change plan.
	Create a plan that outlines the specific actions, tasks, and resources required to implement the change.
Comm change	Communicate & execute change.
	Communicate the change to stakeholders, obtaining buy-in and support, and execute the change plan.
Definition outcome	Define goals & scope of change.
	Clearly define the scope and objectives of the change program and creating a shared understanding of what will be different as a result of the change.

2.1 Definition questions

General overview	During the definition phase of a change program It is important to establish clear roles, responsibilities and expectations for the change program team and stakeholders, and some key questions to consider include:
Problem to address	What is the specific problem or opportunity that the change program aims to address?
Impacted stakeholders	Who will be affected by the change and how?
Desired outcomes	What are the desired outcomes of the change program?
Resources required	What resources (financial, personnel, time) are required to implement the change?
Risk and obstacles	What are the potential risks and obstacles that may arise during the change process?
Key success factors	What are the key success factors for the change program?
Success measures	How will the success of the change program be measured?
Communication & engagement plan	How will stakeholders be engaged and informed throughout the change process?

2.1 Definition process

General overview	The planning phase of a change program typically includes several steps for defining the scope and goals of the change.
The problem for change	Identify the reasons for the change, such as a business need or customer requirement.
The objectives and goals of the change	Specify what the change program aims to achieve as more efficiency, cost savings, improved customer satisfaction.
The scope of the change	Identify the specific areas of the firm that will be affected by the change & outline the boundaries of the change program.
Impacted stakeholders	Identify all the individuals, groups, or organizations that will be impacted by the change and determining their level of involvement in the change program.
Gap analysis	Analyse the current state of the organization and comparing it to the desired future state to identify gaps that need to be closed in order to achieve the change objectives.
Change strategy	Outline a plan for how the change will be executed and managed (timelines, resources, and roles & responsibilities.

2.1 Definition plan components

General overview	The definition plan is a document that outlines the scope, objectives and change strategy of the program.
Problem statement	Describe the reasons for the change &the benefits desired.
Objectives and goals	Outline the program outcomes to achieve as more efficiency, cost savings, or improved customer satisfaction.
Scope	Define the areas of the firm that will be affected by the change and outlines the boundaries of the change program.
Stakeholder analysis	Identify all the individuals or groups that will be impacted by the change and determine their level of involvement in it.
Gap analysis	Analise the ASIS state of the firm and compares it to the TOBE future state to identify the gaps that need to be closed.
Change strategy	Outline the plan for how the change will be executed and managed (timelines, resources, and roles &responsibilities).
Change management team	Identify the individuals responsible for planning and executing the change program and their roles and responsibilities.
Budget and resource plan	Outline the financial &resource requirements for the program, including projected costs and the allocation of resources.
Risk management plan	Outline the potential risks associated with the change program and the strategies in place to mitigate them.
Communication plan	Outline the communication strategy for the change program, (how they will be informed, the frequency & channels).

2.1 Definition best practices

General overview	During the planning phase of a change program, it is important to clearly define the objectives, scope, and expected outcomes of the program. Some best practices for the definition part of the planning phase include:
Stakeholder involvement	Involve key stakeholders in the definition process to ensure buy-in and support for the program.
Thorough ASIS assessment	Conduct a thorough assessment of the current state of the organization to identify areas that need improvement.
SMART goals for the change program	Define measurable and specific goals for the program to ensure progress can be tracked and evaluated.
Potential risks and challenges	Identify and address potential risks and challenges that may arise during the program.
Detailed project plan	Develop a detailed project plan (timelines, resource allocation, & clear roles and responsibilities for stakeholders.
Stakeholder comms	Communicate the objectives and scope of the program to all stakeholders to ensure they are aware of the changes that will take place and how they will be affected.

2.1 Definition risks

General overview	There are several risks that can arise during the definition part of the planning phase of a change program, including:
Lack of stakeholder buy-in & support	Lack of buy-in & support from key stakeholders leading to resistance to change and hinder the program's progress.
Poor assessment of current state	Inadequate assessment of the current state of the firm, which can result in the program addressing the wrong issues.
Unclear or unrealistic goals	Unclear or unrealistic goals and objectives, which can lead to confusion and lack of progress.
Failure to address risks	Failure to identify and address potential risks and challenges, which can lead to unexpected problems and setbacks.
Insufficient resources	Insufficient resources (budget, personnel, and expertise) which can impede the program's progress and lead to delays.
Poor communications	Poor comms and lack of transparency, which can lead to confusion, mistrust, and lack of support from stakeholders.
Lack of flexibility	Lack of flexibility and adaptability, which can impede the ability to respond to changes & obstacles that may arise.
Lack of monitoring	Lack of monitoring and evaluation, which can prevent the program from being adjusted as needed.
Lack of clear comms	Insufficient and/or lack of a clear and concise communication plan, which can lead to lack of understanding and support.
Lack of a dedicated team	Lack of a dedicated team, with the right skills and experience, to lead and execute the change program effectively.

2.1 Definition best practices

General overview	Lessons learned for the definition part of the planning phase of a change program can include:
Stakeholder involvement	The importance of involving key stakeholders early on in the process to ensure buy-in and support for the program.
Thorough ASIS assessment	The need for a thorough assessment of the current state of the organization to identify areas that need improvement and to ensure that the program is addressing the right issues.
SMART goas for the program	Define measurable and specific goals for the program to ensure progress can be tracked and evaluated.
Risks & challenges	The need to identify and address potential risks and challenges that may arise during the program.
Detailed project plan	Develop a detailed project plan with timelines, resource allocation & clear roles & responsibilities for stakeholders.
Stakeholder communications	Communicate the goals & scope of the program to all stakeholders so they are aware of the planned changes.
Need for flexibility and adaptability	The need to be flexible and adaptable to changes and obstacles that may arise during the program.
Progress monitoring & evaluation	Monitor and evaluate the progress of the program regularly and making adjustments as necessary.
Clear comms plan	Have a clear and concise comms plan for all stakeholders
Dedicated team for the change program	Have a dedicated team, with the right skills, to lead and execute the change program effectively.

2.2 People

The purpose of the stakeholder part of the planning phase of a change program is to identify and engage key stakeholders in the change process, in order to gain their buy-in, support, and participation in the program.

The goals of this part of the planning phase include:

- To identify all stakeholders who will be affected by the change program and determine their level of interest and influence.
- To understand the needs, concerns and expectations of the stakeholders, in order to address them effectively.
- To communicate the program goals and scope to all stakeholders, so they are aware of the changes and how they will be affected.
- To involve the stakeholders in the planning and implementation of the program to gain their buy-in.
- To establish a clear and open comms plan with stakeholders, to keep them informed of the progress of the program and to address any issues that may arise.

- Building and maintaining strong relationships with stakeholders throughout the program.
- Managing stakeholders' expectations and addressing their concerns throughout the program.
- Gaining the buy-in and support of the stakeholders for the program.

Not properly identifying and engaging stakeholders during the planning phase of a change program can have several negative impacts, including:

- Lack of buy-in from key stakeholders leading resistance to change.
- Insufficient understanding of the needs, and expectations of the stakeholders.
- Confusion and lack of understanding among stakeholders about the objectives and scope of the program.
- Difficulty in involving stakeholders in the planning and execution of the program.
- Poor communication and lack of transparency leading to confusion and mistrust among stakeholders.

2.2 People activities

Identification	**Identify all the stakeholders.**
	Identify all the stakeholders who will be impacted by the change, including internal and external stakeholders.
Analysis	**Analyse the stakeholders.**
	Analyse the stakeholders to understand their needs, expectations, influence level and support for the change.
Stakeholder map	**Create a map of stakeholders.**
	Create a visual representation of the stakeholders and their relationships to understand how they will be impacted.
Engagement	**Engage with stakeholders.**
	Engage with stakeholders to understand their concerns, expectations, and level of support for the change.
Comms	**Communicate with stakeholders.**
	Communicate effectively with stakeholders throughout the change process to keep them informed, address their concerns, and build support for the change.
People outcome	**Identify the stakeholders.**
	Identify all the individuals & groups, who will be affected by the change & determine their level of influence and interest.

2.2 People questions

General overview	During the stakeholder part of the planning phase of a change program, it is important to identify and engage key stakeholders in the change process. Answering these questions will help to ensure that the stakeholders' perspectives are taken into account and that the change program is designed and implemented in a way that addresses their needs, concerns, and expectations. Some key questions to consider when doing this include:
Impacted stakeholder	Who are the stakeholders impacted by the change?
Stakeholder needs	What are the needs, and expectations of the stakeholders?
The type of impact	How will the stakeholders be affected by the change?
Stakeholder involvement	How can we involve the stakeholders in the planning and implementation of the program?
Communication of goals and scope	How can we communicate the objectives and scope of the program to the stakeholders effectively?
Stakeholder relations	How can we build and maintain strong relationships with stakeholders throughout the program?

2.2 People questions

Expectations management	How can we manage stakeholders' expectations and address their concerns throughout the program?
Ways to gain buy-in and support	How can we gain the buy-in and support of the stakeholders for the change program?
Strategic goal alignment	How can we align the program with the strategic direction of the organization?
Risk management of risks & challenges	How can we identify and mitigate potential risks and challenges that may arise during the program?
Effective feedback process	How to make sure that the stakeholders' voices and feedback are heard and considered throughout the change program?
Program status updates	How to ensure that the stakeholders are kept informed about program progress and any changes or issues that may arise?
Decision-making process & governance	What are the key decision-making processes and governance structures that need to be in place to involve the stakeholders in the change program?
Stakeholder engagement metrics	How can we evaluate the effectiveness of our stakeholder engagement efforts and make adjustments as needed?

2.2 People plan components

General overview	A stakeholder plan is a key part of the planning phase of a change program and including these components in the stakeholder plan, firms can ensure that the stakeholders' perspectives are taken into account and that the change program is designed and implemented in a way that addresses their needs, concerns, and expectations.
Stakeholder identification	Identify all stakeholders who will be affected by the change program and determine their level of interest and influence.
Stakeholder analysis	Understand the needs, concerns, and expectations of the stakeholders to address them effectively.
Communication plan	Develop a clear and open communication plan with stakeholders, to keep them informed of the progress of the program and to address any issues that may arise.
Stakeholder engagement	Involve stakeholders in the planning and implementation of the program, in order to gain their buy-in and support.
Relationship management	Build and maintain strong relationships with stakeholders throughout the program.

2.2 People plan best practices

Expectations management	Manage stakeholders' expectations and addressing their concerns throughout the program.
Governance and decision-making	Outline the key decision-making processes and governance structures to involve the stakeholders in the change program.
Evaluation and adjustment	Establish a mechanism to evaluate the effectiveness of the stakeholder engagement efforts and adjust as needed.
Risks and challenges	Identify and mitigate potential risks and challenges that may arise during the program, specifically related to stakeholders.
Alignment with strategy	Ensure that the program is aligned with the strategic direction of the organization.
Feedback and participation	Encourage stakeholders to provide feedback and participation throughout the change program
Communication and reporting	Having a clear and consistent communication and reporting plan to ensure stakeholders are informed and updated on the progress of the change program.

2.2 People risks

General overview	There are several risks associated with the stakeholder engagement aspect of a change program, including:
Resistance to change	Stakeholders may resist the proposed changes, which can slow down or even halt the program.
Misaligned expectations	Stakeholders may have different expectations and goals for the program, leading to confusion and potential conflict.
Lack of buy-in	If stakeholders do not support the changes, they may not fully commit to the program leading to poor execution & outcomes.
Limited engagement	If not, enough stakeholders are engaged in the planning process, key perspectives and considerations may be missed, leading to a less effective program.
Communication breakdown	Poor communication with stakeholders can lead to confusion, mistrust and lack of support for the program.
Limited resources	Engaging stakeholders can be resource-intensive, and if not managed effectively, can consume a significant portion of the project budget and timeline.

2.2 People lessons learned

General overview	There are several key lessons that can be learned from managing stakeholder engagement during the planning phase of a change program, including:
Involve stakeholders early	Involving stakeholders early in the planning process can help to build buy-in and ensure that their perspectives and concerns are taken into account.
Communicate effectively	Clear, frequent, and transparent communication is essential for building trust and understanding among stakeholders.
Manage expectations	Managing stakeholders' expectations and goals can help to align them with the program and minimize resistance.
Address resistance	Anticipate and address resistance to change early on, by involving key stakeholders in the planning process and addressing their concerns.
Tailor engagement	Different stakeholders may require different levels and types of engagement, so it's important to tailor engagement efforts to meet the needs of each group.
Monitor and adjust	Continuously monitor and adjust stakeholder engagement efforts as the program progresses to ensure that they remain effective and aligned with the program's goals.
Be prepared for unexpected changes	Be ready to adapt to unexpected changes in stakeholder engagement and respond accordingly.

2.3 Readiness

The specific goals and objectives of the readiness component can vary depending on the change program and the firm, but some common goals are:

- Identify the current capabilities, processes, and systems that will be affected by the change, and determining the gaps that need to be filled to ensure the change is successful.
- Identify potential risks and barriers to the change and developing a plan to mitigate them.
- Build support and buy-in for the change among stakeholders, including employees, managers, and other key stakeholders.
- Develop a communication plan that clearly communicates the goals, objectives and benefits of the change program to all stakeholders.
- Identify the resources that will be needed to implement the change program, such as funding, personnel, and technology and develop a plan to obtain them.

- Engage employees early in the process to know their concerns & build their commitment to the change.
- Prepare for the actual execution of the change program, by developing detailed implementation plans, training employees, and testing the new processes or systems.

Not properly conducting the readiness component in the planning phase of a change program can lead to several negative impacts, including:

- Without proper assessment of the current state, risks and barriers may not be identified, leading to problems during the implementation.
- Without proper planning, necessary resources such as funding, personnel, or technology may not be available, leading to delays and potential failure of the program.
- Without proper readiness, the change program may not achieve its goals and objectives and may not deliver the expected results and benefits.

2.3 Readiness workstream activities

Capabilities	**Assess ASIS capabilities.**
	Evaluate the current skills, resources, and processes of the firm to determine its current level of readiness for change.
Gaps	**Identify gaps.**
	Identify gaps between the organization's current capabilities and what is required to successfully implement the change.
Culture	**Assess firm's culture**
	Assessing the firm's culture to understand the level of resistance to change & the degree of support for the change.
Resistance	**Assess change resistance.**
	Identify potential resistance to the change and developing strategies to address it.
Change team	**Identify & assemble team.**
	Identify and assemble a cross functional team of stakeholders that will be responsible for leading and managing the change effort.
Readiness outcome	**Assess firm readiness.**
	Assess the current readiness of the firm and stakeholders to undertake the change, & identifying any potential resistance.

2.3 Readiness questions

General overview	During the planning phase of a change program, it is important to assess the readiness of the firm for the proposed changes. Some questions to assess readiness include:
Current awareness	What's the current awareness level of the change program?
Stakeholders feelings	How do the stakeholders feel about the proposed changes?
Barriers to execution	Are there any perceived or actual barriers to the change?
Resources required	What resources, including funding, personnel, and technology, will be required to implement the changes?
Comms & rollout	How will the changes be communicated & rolled out?
Support & training requirements	What support and training will be needed for employees to effectively transition to the new changes?
Progress metrics	How will the progress be measured and evaluated?
Resistance to change	How will resistance to change be managed and addressed?
Risk management	What are the risks involved with the change?
Sustainability plan	What is the plan for maintaining the change &sustainability?

2.3 Readiness plan components

General overview	A readiness plan is an important component of the planning phase of a change program, as it helps to ensure that the firm is prepared to successfully implement the proposed changes.
Communication and engagement	:A plan for effectively communicating the proposed changes to all relevant stakeholders(staff, customers, stakeholders)
Training and development	A plan for providing the necessary training and development to employees to effectively transition to the new changes.
Resources and logistics	A plan for acquiring and allocating the needed resources (funding, personnel & technology) to execute the program.
Resistance management	A plan for identifying and managing resistance to change, including strategies for addressing any concerns.
Impact assessment	An assessment of the potential impact of the changes on different parts of the firm & any potential risks or challenges.
Measurement and evaluation	A plan to measure and evaluate the progress and success of the changes, including metrics and KPIs.
Stakeholder management	A plan for engaging with key stakeholders (staff, customers, and stakeholder for their buy-in and support for the changes.
Continuity plan	A plan for maintaining the changes and for sustainability, & strategies for addressing any post execution challenges.
Rollout plan	A plan for the phased rollout of the changes to minimize disruption and ensure a smooth transition.
Governance	A plan for governance and oversight of the change program (clear roles and an incident management plan.

2.3 Readiness go-live plan components

Scope & objectives of go-live plan	Define the scope and objectives of the go-live plan, including the specific systems, processes, and people that will be impacted by the change.
Detailed execution plan	Develop a detailed implementation schedule, including specific milestones, deadlines, and dependencies.
Assign roles & responsibilities	Identify and assign specific roles and responsibilities for all team members involved in the go-live process.
Thorough testing plan	Develop a thorough testing plan to ensure that all systems and processes are functioning correctly before go-live.
Comprehensive training plan	Develop a comprehensive training plan for all employees who will be impacted by the change.
Comms plan	Develop a comms plan to ensure that all stakeholders are informed of the go-live schedule & changes that may occur.
Risk management	Identify and plan for potential risks and contingencies, including a rollback plan in case of unexpected issues.
PIR review	Develop a post-implementation review plan to evaluate the success of the go-live and identify areas for improvement.
Post monitor & maintain plan	Develop a plan to monitor and maintain the new systems and processes after go-live.
Dedicated go-live support team	Assemble a dedicated go-live support team to provide assistance during the transition.

2.3 Readiness best practices

Identify & assess potential impact	Identify and assess the potential impact of the change on the organization and its stakeholders.
Comms plan	Develop a communication plan to keep stakeholders informed and engaged throughout the change process.
Realistic timeline	Establish a clear and realistic timeline for the change.
Resistance to change	Identify and address any potential resistance to the change.
Training plan	Develop a training plan to ensure that all employees have the necessary skills to support the change.
Success criteria	Establish a clear and measurable set of success criteria.
Post evaluation for effectiveness	Establish a post-change evaluation process to measure the effectiveness of the change & identify areas for improvement.
Sustainability	Create a support structure so the change is sustainable
Identify KPIs	Identify key performance indicators to track progress.
Continuously monitor & adjust	Continuously monitor and adjust the readiness plan as needed throughout the change process.

2.3 Readiness risks

Resistance to change	Employees may be resistant to the change, which can slow down or impede progress.
Lack of clear communication	If stakeholders are not informed or engaged throughout the change process, they may become confused or disengaged.
Inadequate training	When staff do not have the necessary skills to support the change, it may be difficult for them to adapt.
Unrealistic expectations:	If the goals of the change are not clearly defined or are unrealistic, it can lead to disappointment and frustration.
Limited resources	Without sufficient resources, it can be difficult to implement the change effectively.
Lack of support from key stakeholders	If key stakeholders are not fully committed to the change, it may be difficult to gain the necessary support and buy-in.
Technical issues	Technical issues can cause delays or impede progress.
Insufficient testing	If the systems and processes are not thoroughly tested before implementation, it may lead to unexpected problems.
Inability to measure success	Without clear and measurable success criteria, it may be difficult to determine if the change was successful.
Sustainability challenges	Without proper planning and support, it may be difficult to sustain the change over time.

2.3 Readiness lessons learned

Involve stakeholders early in the process	Involve stakeholders early on in the change process to ensure their buy-in and support.
Communicate effectively	Communicate effectively & frequently with stakeholders to keep them informed & engaged during the change process.
Training & development	Provide training and development opportunities for employees to help them adapt to the change.
Realistic timeframe & resource needs	Be realistic about the timeline and resources required for the change, and make adjustments as needed.
Address resistance to change	Address potential resistance to the change by identifying and addressing the underlying concerns of those affected.
Clear success criteria	Establish clear and measurable success criteria to evaluate the effectiveness of the change.
Continuously monitor the progress	Continuously monitor the progress of the change and make adjustments as needed to ensure it stays on track.
Sustainability plan	Develop a plan to sustain the change over time, including monitoring and maintenance.
Conduct a post-change evaluation	Conduct a post-change evaluation to identify areas for improvement and to inform future change initiatives.
Learn from previous change initiatives	Learn from previous change initiatives and apply the lessons learned to future changes.

2.4 Comms Plan

The purpose of a communications plan in the planning phase of a strategic organization change management program is to ensure that all stakeholders are informed and engaged throughout the change process.

The objectives of the plan may include:

- Identifying key stakeholders and understanding their needs, concerns, and expectations
- Communicating the reasons for the change and its expected benefits
- Keeping stakeholders informed of progress and addressing any issues.
- Building support and buy-in for the change
- Managing resistance and addressing any potential conflicts
- Ensuring clear, consistent and timely communication
- Aligning the communications plan with overall change strategy.
- Evaluating the effectiveness of the communications plan and making adjustments as needed.

The goal of the communications plan is to create a shared understanding of the change and its implications among all stakeholders, and to help facilitate a smooth and successful transition to the new state.

Not having a communications plan in the planning phase of a strategic organization change management program can have a number of negative impacts, such as:

- Without a clear and consistent communication strategy, stakeholders may not fully understand the reasons for the change or its expected benefits, leading to confusion and mistrust.
- Stakeholders who feel uninformed or left out of the process may be more likely to resist the change, making it more difficult to achieve buy-in and support.
- Without a plan for communicating progress and addressing any issues or concerns, the change process may be slowed down by unexpected obstacles.

Overall, a lack of communications plan can lead to poor implementation of the change program, low adoption and less chances of achieving the desired outcomes.

2.4 Comms plan workstream activities

Stakeholders	Identify key stakeholders.
	Determine who the key stakeholders are and what their interests and concerns are in relation to the change.
Comms strategy	Develop a comms strategy
	Based on the identified stakeholders and their needs, develop a communication strategy that outlines the methods and channels that will be used to communicate with them.
Messaging	Create clear messaging.
	Develop clear and consistent messaging that is tailored to the specific stakeholders and their interests and concerns.
Schedule	Create a comms schedule.
	Plan and schedule regular communication activities, such as meetings, updates, and training, to ensure stakeholders are informed and engaged throughout the change process.
Evaluation	Evaluate and adjust comms plan.
	Continuously evaluate the effectiveness of the comms plan and adjust as needed so that stakeholders are effectively engaged and that the change is implemented successfully.
Comms plan outcome	Develop comms plan for change.
	Create a plan to communicate and engage with stakeholders throughout the change process.

2.4 Comms plan questions

General overview	Some key questions to consider when planning the communications aspect of a change program include:
Key stakeholders	Who are the key stakeholders that need to be informed and engaged throughout the change process?
Stakeholders information needs	What information do these stakeholders need to know and when do they need to know it?
Comms channels to stakeholders	How will we communicate with these stakeholders (e.g. email, town hall meetings, newsletters)?
Comms owner	Who will be responsible for creating and disseminating the communications?
Comms metrics	How to measure the effectiveness of our communications ?
Resistance approach	How will you handle resistance during the change process?
Firm alignment	How will you align the change with the firm's vision & values?
Comms inclusivity	How will you ensure that the change is communicated in a way that is inclusive and accessible to all employees?
Staff informed and engaged	How will you keep the employees informed and engaged throughout the change process?

2.4 Comms plan components

General overview	A communications plan includes the following components:
Stakeholder analysis	Identify the key stakeholders that need to be informed and engaged throughout the change process (estaff, managers, customers, suppliers, and other external stakeholders).
Communications objectives	Clearly define the information needed to be communicated, to whom, and when, in order to support the change program.
Message development	Develop clear, concise, and consistent messages that will be used to communicate the change program to stakeholders.
Communications channels	Identify the best channels for communicating with stakeholders (email, newsletters, intranet, town halls).
Communications calendar	Develop a timeline for the comms activities, including key milestones and deadlines so that information is timely.
Creation & execution	Assign role for creating & executing the comms plan.
Evaluation and feedback	Set up a process to measure the effectiveness of the comms and gathering feedback from stakeholders.
Contingency planning	Identify potential risks and issues that may arise.
Managing resistance	Develop a plan to handle resistance and objections.
Aligning change with firm's vision &values	Make sure that the change is communicated in a way that is aligned with the company's vision and values.

2.4 Comms plan best practices

General overview	When creating a comms plan as part of the planning phase in a change program, it is important to consider the following:
Define goals & align with change program	Clearly define the goals of the communications plan, and align them with the overall objectives of the change program.
Key stakeholders with tailored messages	Identify the key stakeholders and target audiences for the comms and tailor the messaging and channels accordingly.
Detailed comms schedule	Develop a detailed timeline for the communications plan, including key milestones and deadlines.
Clear & consistent messaging	Establish a clear and consistent message that is easy to understand and communicate.
Variety of comms channels	Utilize a variety of communication channels to reach all stakeholders (email, company intranet, town hall meetings).
Continuously monitor comms effectiveness	Continuously monitor and evaluate the effectiveness of the communications plan, and make adjustments as needed.
Comms plan is integrated in program	Ensure that the comms plan is integrated with the change management plan and it is aligned with the change strategy.
Crisis management plan	Have a crisis management plan (comms strategies for handling unexpected events or issues that may arise)
Designated person for comms activities	Have a designated person responsible for overseeing and managing the comms plan with the necessary resources.

2.4 Comms plan risks

General overview	When creating a comms plan as part of the planning phase in a change program, there are several risks to consider:
Miscommunication	The message may not be clear or consistent, leading to confusion and misunderstanding among stakeholders.
Lack of buy-in	Stakeholders may not be fully engaged in the program if they don't understand the purpose or benefits of the comms plan.
Resistance to change	Stakeholders may be resistant to the changes & the comms plan may not effectively address their concerns or objections.
Inadequate timing	The timing of the comms may be inappropriate, causing stakeholders to miss important info or announcements.
Limited reach	The comms plan may not reach all stakeholders, or may not be tailored to the specific needs of certain target audiences.
Failure to evaluate	Not evaluating the effectiveness of the comms plan can lead to lack of progress in the change program.
Inadequate resources	Insufficient resources as budget and personnel, may limit the ability to effectively execute the communications plan.
Insufficient crisis management	The lack of a crisis management plan or the inability to effectively communicate during a crisis can lead to confusion,
Limited ownership	Without a designated person responsible for overseeing the comms plan, the plan may not be executed effectively.

2.4 Comms plan lessons learned

General overview	When creating a comms plan as part of the planning phase in a change program, keep these lessons learned in mind:
Define goals and align with change program	Clearly define the goals of the comms plan, and align them with the overall objectives of the change program.
Identify stakeholders & tailor messaging	Identify the key stakeholders and target audiences for the comms, and tailor the messaging and channels accordingly.
Detailed comms schedule	Develop a detailed timeline for the communications plan, including key milestones and deadlines.
Clear & consistent messaging	Establish a clear and consistent message that is easy to understand and communicate.
Use a variety of comms channels	Utilize a variety of communication channels to reach all stakeholders, including email, company intranet, town hall meetings, and individual or group meetings.
Continually monitor and evaluate comms	Continuously monitor and evaluate the effectiveness of the communications plan, and make adjustments as needed.

2.4 Comms plan lessons learned

Comms plan is integrated & aligned	Ensure that the comms plan is integrated with the overall change management plan and that it is aligned with the change management strategy.
Crisis management plan in place	Have a crisis management plan in place, including communication strategies for handling unexpected events or issues that may arise during the change program.
Designated person for comms	Have a designated person responsible for overseeing and managing the communications plan, and give them the necessary resources and support to do so.
Listen to feedback & open to changes	Listen to feedback and be open to changes in the communication plan as the change program progresses.
Communicate regularly	Communicate regularly and transparently with all stakeholders throughout the change program
Communicate the change benefits	Communicate the benefits of the change program and the reasons why it is necessary.
Use storytelling & visual aids	Use storytelling and visual aids to make the communications more engaging and impactful.
Be prepared for resistance to change	Be prepared to address any resistance to change through effective communication strategies.

2.5 Governance

The purpose of governance as part of the planning phase in a change program is to establish a framework for decision-making, oversight, and accountability for the change initiative. Governance is essential for ensuring that the change program is aligned with the firm's overall strategy, that it is executed effectively, and that it delivers the intended benefits.

The goals and objectives of governance as part of a change program include:

- To ensure that the change program is aligned with the organization's strategic goals and that it supports the business direction.
- To help to identify and manage risks and issues that may arise during the change program, and to implement appropriate mitigation strategies.
- To provide a framework for decision-making, and ensures that the right decisions are made at the right time, & by the right people.

- To ensure that the change program complies with relevant laws, regulations, and standards, and that it meets the organization's own policies and procedures.
- To promote transparency and accountability, and ensures that stakeholders are informed of the progress and outcomes of the change program.
- To ensure that the changes made during the change program are sustainable, and that they do not negatively impact the firm's future operations.

Poor governance as part of the planning phase in a change program can have several negative impacts on the organization, including:

- It can lead to a lack of alignment between the change program and the firm's overall strategy.
- Poor governance can lead to a lack of oversight and accountability, which can result in the change program being executed poorly or not at all.

2.5 Governance activities

Team	**Establish a governance team.**
	Create a team responsible for overseeing the change management process so it aligns with the firm's goals.
Roles	**Define roles & responsibilities.**
	Clearly define the roles and responsibilities of the governance team & other stakeholders involved in the change process.
Decisions	**Develop decision-making process.**
	Establish protocols for decision-making and problem-solving, such as a clear process for escalating issues and disputes.
Metrics	**Create metrics for performance.**
	Develop metrics to measure the performance of the change management process and the success of the change itself.
Reviews	**Regularly review & update.**
	Regularly review and update the governance structure to ensure it remains effective and aligned with the firm's goals. so that the governance structure can be responsive to change & adapt to new requirements as they arise.
Governance outcome	**Establish change governance.**
	Establish a governance structure to oversee the change program (roles, responsibilities, and decision-making).

2.5 Governance questions

Goals & objectives	What are the goals & objectives of the change program?
Impacted stakeholders	Who are the stakeholders that will be affected by the change, and how will their needs be addressed?
Decision process	How will decisions be made & by whom during the program?
Monitor processes & systems	What processes and systems will be put in place to monitor and measure the success of the change program?
Risk management	How will risks be identified & managed during the program?
Communications plan	How will comms be handled during the change program to ensure all stakeholders are informed and engaged?
Change program integration	How will the change program be integrated with existing governance structures and processes?
Compliance & regulatory needs	How will compliance and regulatory requirements be addressed during the change program?

2.5 Governance plan components

Governance structure	The governance structure should clearly define roles, responsibilities and decision-making authority for all stakeholders involved in the change program.
Policy and Procedures	The governance plan should include policies and procedures that will be followed during the change program (decision-making processes, risk management, and communications)
Performance Metrics	Develop metrics to measure the performance and success of the change program. These metrics should be aligned with the overall goals and objectives of the change program.
Risk Management	Create a risk management strategy that identifies potential risks and outlines measures to mitigate or manage them.
Compliance and Regulation	Determine measures to ensure compliance with relevant laws, regulations and industry standards
Communication Plan	Develop a comms plan that outlines how stakeholders will be informed and engaged during the change program.
Continual Monitoring and Review	Develop a process for monitoring program progress and for conducting regular reviews to identify areas for improvement.
Accountability and Responsibilities	Clearly define the roles, responsibilities, and accountability of all stakeholders involved in the change program.

2.5 Governance best practices

Establish clear goals and objectives	The governance plan should be aligned with the overall goals and objectives of the change program.
Involve stakeholders	Develop the governance plan with input from all relevant stakeholders so that their needs & concerns are noted.
Define roles and responsibilities	Clearly define roles, responsibilities and decision-making authority for all stakeholders involved in the change program.
Establish metrics	Develop metrics to measure the performance and success of the change program. These metrics should be aligned with the overall goals and objectives of the change program.
Risk management	Create a risk management strategy that identifies potential risks and outlines measures to mitigate or manage them.
Compliance	Determine measures to ensure compliance with relevant laws, regulations and industry standards
Communication	Develop a communication plan that outlines how stakeholders will be informed and engaged during the change program.
Continual monitoring and review	Create a process for monitoring the progress of the program & conduct regular reviews to identify improvement areas.
Flexibility	The governance plan should be flexible enough to adapt to changes as the program progresses.
Accountability	Clearly define the roles, responsibilities, and accountability of all stakeholders involved in the change program, and ensure that they are aware of and understand their roles.

2.5 Governance risks

Poor stakeholder engagement	If key stakeholders are not properly engaged during the planning phase of a change program, they may resist or oppose the change, leading to delays and increased costs.
Lack of clear governance structure	Without a clear governance structure, roles and responsibilities may be poorly defined, leading to confusion.
Insufficient risk management	If risks are not identified and addressed during the planning phase, they may negatively impact the change program.
Lack of communication	Poor comms can lead to misunderstandings and mistrust among stakeholders, hindering the success of the program.
Noncompliance	If regulatory and compliance requirements are not properly considered during the planning phase, the change program may be at risk of noncompliance.
Lack of accountability	Clear accountability and responsibility, is required as it can be difficult to ensure that the change program stays on track and meets its goals and objectives.
Inadequate performance metrics	Appropriate performance metrics are needed as it can be difficult to measure the success of the change program and identify areas for improvement.
Resistance to change	Some stakeholders may have resistance to change, which can slow down the program if not properly managed
Lack of flexibility	If the governance plan is too rigid and inflexible, it may be difficult to adapt to changes as the program progresses.

2.5 Governance lessons learned

Scope & goals	Clearly defining the scope and goals of the change program.
Current state of the organisation	Understanding the current state of the organization and identifying areas for improvement.
Inputs & buy-in from stakeholders	Gathering input and buy-in from key stakeholders, including employees, management, and other relevant parties.
Detailed execution plan	Developing a detailed plan for implementing the change, including timelines, resources, and milestones.
Risk management	Identifying and mitigating potential risks and challenges associated with the change.
Communications	Communicating the change effectively to all stakeholders.
Continuous monitoring & evaluation	Continuously monitoring and evaluating the progress of the change program to make adjustments as needed.

EDUCATING THE MIND WITHOUT EDUCATING THE HEART IS NO EDUCATION AT ALL.

Aristotle

3.0 Execution

The primary goal of the implementation phase in a change management program is to put the plan developed during the planning phase into action.

This includes executing the tasks and activities identified in the plan, as well as addressing any issues or challenges that arise during the implementation process. The implementation phase also includes ensuring that all stakeholders are informed and involved in the process and that the changes are being implemented as intended. The goal of this phase is to successfully implement the changes in the organization and realise the benefits of the change management program.

Ensuring that the change is implemented in a controlled and coordinated manner.

- Communicate the change effectively to all stakeholders
- Ensure that the change is embedded and sustained within the organization
- Meet the agreed upon timelines and budgets for the change program.

The 5 key components and associated activities for the execution phase of a change management program are:

1. Provide training, education and other resources to stakeholders to prepare them for the change.
2. Execute the plan for change, including any necessary process changes, IT system updates, or other technical requirements.
3. Identify and manage any resistance to change from stakeholders.
4. Regularly communicate progress on the change program to stakeholders and addressing any concerns or issues that arise.
5. Make sure the change becomes part of organization's normal way of doing things, and that it is fully integrated into the firm's culture and processes

3.0 Execution Plan Linkages

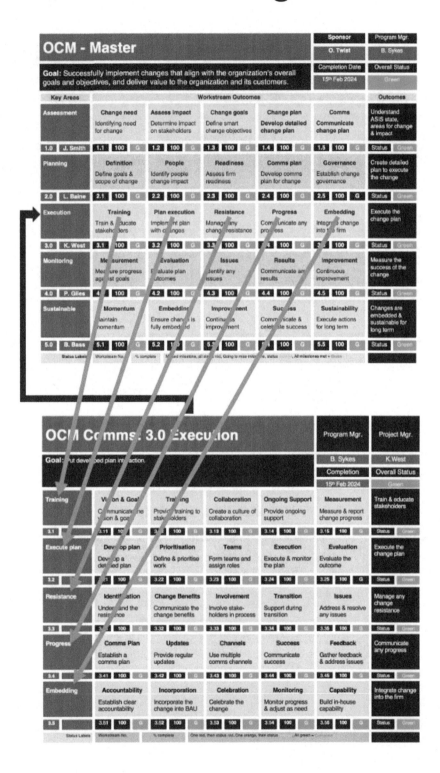

3.0 Execution Workstream Plan

OCM Comms: 3.0 Execution						Program Mgr.	Project Mgr.
Goal: Put developed plan into action.						B. Sykes	K.West
						Completion	Overall Status
						15th Feb 2024	Green
Training	**Vision & Goals** Communicate the vision & goals	**Training** Provide training to stakeholders	**Collaboration** Create a culture of collaboration	**Ongoing Support** Provide ongoing support	**Measurement** Measure & report change progress		Train & educate stakeholders
3.1	3.11 100 G	3.12 100 G	3.13 100 G	3.14 100 G	3.15 100 G		Status Green
Execute plan	**Develop plan** Develop a detailed plan	**Prioritisation** Define & prioritise work	**Teams** Form teams and assign roles	**Execution** Execute & monitor the plan	**Evaluation** Evaluate the outcome		Execute the change plan
3.2	3.21 100 G	3.22 100 G	3.23 100 G	3.24 100 G	3.25 100 G		Status Green
Resistance	**Identification** Understand the resistance	**Change Benefits** Communicate the change benefits	**Involvement** Involve stake-holders in process	**Transition** Support during transition	**Issues** Address & resolve any issues		Manage any change resistance
3.3	3.31 100 G	3.32 100 G	3.33 100 G	3.34 100 G	3.35 100 G		Status Green
Progress	**Comms Plan** Establish a comms plan	**Updates** Provide regular updates	**Channels** Use multiple comms channels	**Success** Communicate success	**Feedback** Gather feedback & address issues		Communicate any progress
3.4	3.41 100 G	3.42 100 G	3.43 100 G	3.44 100 G	3.45 100 G		Status Green
Embedding	**Accountability** Establish clear accountability	**Incorporation** Incorporate the change into BAU	**Celebration** Celebrate the change	**Monitoring** Monitor progress & adjust as need	**Capability** Build in-house capability		Integrate change into the firm
3.5	3.51 100 G	3.52 100 G	3.53 100 G	3.54 100 G	3.55 100 G		Status Green
Status Labels	Workstream No.	% complete	One red, then status red, One orange, then status orange, All green = Complete				

3.1 Training

The purpose of the training component of the execution phase of a change program is to equip employees with the knowledge, skills, and abilities they need to effectively and efficiently perform their roles in the new environment created by the change. The objectives and goals of this training may include:

- Ensure that employees understand the change and its rationale
- Provide staff with the information and tools they need to perform their roles in the new environment
- Build employee confidence and competence in the new processes, systems, and technologies
- Reduce resistance to change by providing employees with the support they need to adapt to the new environment.
- Enhance the overall effectiveness of the change by ensuring that employees are prepared to take on their new roles and responsibilities

Poor training during the execution phase of a change program can have several negative impacts, including:

- Without adequate training, employees may struggle to understand and perform their new roles and responsibilities, leading to decreased productivity.
- Poor training can lead to employee confusion, frustration, and lack of confidence, which can in turn increase resistance to the change.
- Staff may not have the knowledge and skills they need to perform their jobs correctly, leading to an increased likelihood of errors and mistakes.
- Decreased employee engagement and motivation which can in turn lead to decreased employee engagement and commitment to the change.
- Can lead to employees feeling unprepared for their new roles and may result in them seeking new employment.
- The implementation of the change can be delayed as employees are not ready to perform their new roles, which can cause delays and additional costs.

3.1 Training workstream activities

Vision & goals	Communicate the vision & goals.
	It is important to clearly communicate the purpose and goals of the program to stakeholders, so they understand why the change is necessary and what benefits it will bring.
Training	Provide training to stakeholders.
	Provide training on the proposed changes and educate them.
Collaboration	Create a culture of collaboration.
	Establishing a culture of collaboration and continuous improvement to emphasise teamwork and the need for constant adaptation to changing requirements.
Ongoing support	Provide ongoing support.
	It is important to provide ongoing support and coaching to help them overcome challenges working in the new way and continue to improve their skills.
Measurement	Measure & report progress.
	To ensure the success of the change program, it is key to track progress and measure the impact of the changes. This data can be used to identify areas for improvement.
Training outcome	Train & educate stakeholders.
	Provide training, education and other resources to stakeholders to prepare them for the change.

3.1 Training questions

General overview	Some key questions to consider for training as part of the execution phase of a change program include:
Training requirements	What training is required for different groups of individuals (e.g. staff, managers, leaders) to eimplement the change?
Training delivery	Training delivery method (e.g. online, in-person, self-paced)?
Training role	Who will be responsible for delivering the training?
Success criteria	How to evaluate the value of the training & measure it?
Training gaps	How will any gaps in training be identified and addressed?
Training integration into overall timeline	How will the training be integrated into the overall change plan and timeline?
Sustainability	How will it be sustained after the training is completed?
Training alignment to learning strategy	How will the training be aligned with the firm's learning and development strategy?
Training customisation	How will the training be customized to the specific needs of the organization and its employees?

3.1 Training plan components

General overview	The core components for a training plan as part of the execution phase of a change program include:
Objectives	Clearly defined and measurable objectives for the training, aligned with the overall goals of the change program.
Audience	Identification of the specific groups of individuals who will be required to receive training, and their specific training needs.
Content	Development of training materials and content, including instructional design and lesson plans.
Delivery method	Selection of the best delivery method for the training (e.g. online, in-person, self-paced) and logistics for its execution.
Evaluation	Develop a plan to evaluate the effectiveness of the training, including metrics and methods for measuring success.
Sustainment	The plan to sustain the learning after the training is completed (follow-up sessions, reinforcement, coaching).
Alignment	Alignment of the training plan with the organization's overall change plan and timeline.
Resources	Identify resources (financial, personnel, technology, etc.) required for successful implementation of the training plan.
Communication	A plan for communicating the training plan and its implementation to all stakeholders (staff & leaders).

3.1 Training best practices

Involve staff and stakeholders	Involve staff and stakeholders in the training development process so that it meets their needs and addresses concerns.
Make the training relevant and engaging	Use real-world examples and scenarios, interactive activities, and case studies to make the training relevant and engaging.
Provide opportunities for practice	Provide opportunities for staff to practice new skills and receive feedback to help them apply what they've learned.
Use a blended learning approach	Use a blended learning approach that combines different training methods, such as online, in-person, and self-paced, to meet the different learning styles of employees.
Evaluate and adjust the training as needed	Continuously evaluate the training and make adjustments as needed to ensure its effectiveness.
Communicate the training plan	Communicate the training plan and its implementation to all stakeholders, including employees, managers, and leaders.
Make it part of the culture	Incorporate the training into the organizational culture and make it an ongoing process, not just a one-time event.
Leverage technology	Use technology to enhance the training experience and support continued learning.
Align with the firm's learning strategy	Align the training plan with the organization's overall learning and development strategy to ensure that it fits within the organization's broader plans for employee development.

3.1 Training risks

General overview	There are several risks associated with training as part of the execution phase of a change program, including:
Insufficient buy-in from staff and stakeholders	If staff and stakeholders do not see the value in the training, they may be resistant to participating in the training.
Limited resources	Insufficient resources as funding, people, or technology, can impede the development and delivery of effective training.
Inadequate training content	Training content that is not relevant, engaging, or detailed enough may not effectively prepare staff for the change.
Limited opportunities for practice	Without opportunities for staff to practice new skills and receive feedback, they may struggle to apply learnings.
Lack of follow-up and reinforcement	Without follow-up and reinforcement, staff may struggle to retain what they've learned and may not fully implement it.
Difficulty in measuring training effectiveness	It may be hard to measure the effectiveness of the training, making it difficult to determine if it has been successful.
Inconsistency in the delivery of the training	Inconsistency in the delivery of the training, such as different trainers teaching the same material in different ways, can result in confusion among staff and a lack of standardization.
Resistance to change	Some employees may be resistant to change and may not fully participate in the training, which could be seen as a risk for the overall change program.
Limited comms	Limited comms regarding the training plan and its execution can lead to confusion and mistrust among staff.

3.1 Training lessons learned

Involve staff in the training development	Involving employees and other stakeholders in the training development process can help to ensure that the training meets their needs and addresses their concerns.
Use relevant, engaging training content	Use real-world examples, interactive activities, and case studies can make the training more relevant and engaging.
The value of practice and feedback	Providing opportunities for employees to practice new skills & receive feedback can help them apply what they've learned.
Follow-up and reinforcement	Follow-up and reinforcement can help employees retain what they've learned and fully implement the change.
Effective evaluation and measurement	Develop a plan to evaluate the effectiveness of the training, including metrics and methods for measuring progress and success, can help determine if adjustments are needed.
Consistency in delivery	Ensuring consistency in the delivery of the training can help to avoid confusion among staff and promote standardization.
The need for communication	Communicating the training plan and its implementation to all stakeholders, including employees, managers, and leaders can help to build trust and understanding.
The importance of sustainability	Making the training an ongoing process & include it into the firm's culture can help to sustain the change over time.
Align training with the overall change plan	Align the training plan with the firm's overall change plan and timeline can help ensure that it is integrated and supports the overall goals of the change program.

3.2 Execution Plan

The purpose of an implementation plan in the execute phase of a change program is to outline the specific actions and tasks that need to be completed in order to successfully implement the changes outlined in the previous planning phases. The goals of the implementation plan are to ensure that the change is smoothly integrated into the organization and that it meets the objectives that were set out in the planning phase. The objectives of the implementation plan may include:

- Clearly defining roles and responsibilities for those involved in the implementation
- Establishing a timeline for the implementation
- Identifying and addressing any potential risks or obstacles to the implementation
- Communicating the change to stakeholders and ensuring that they are on board with the plan
- Measuring the success of the implementation and making adjustments as necessary.

A poor implementation plan can have a number of negative impacts on a change program. Some of these impacts include:

- A poor implementation plan can result in delays in the implementation of the change, which can lead to missed deadlines and a loss of momentum.
- Poor planning can lead to additional costs, such as the need to redo work that was not done correctly the first time.
- Without a clear plan in place, it can be difficult to measure the success of the change and make adjustments as necessary, which can result in the change not having the desired impact.
- If stakeholders are not communicated with effectively or feel that the change is not being implemented in a way that is beneficial to them, they may lose buy-in for the change.
- A poor implementation plan can lead to increased resistance to the change from employees, which can make it more difficult to implement.

3.2 Execution plan workstream activities

Develop plan	**Develop a detailed plan.**
	Develop a detailed plan that outlines the steps that need to be taken to achieve the desired outcome. This plan includes goals, timelines, resource requirements, and key milestones.
Prioritisation	**Define & prioritize work.**
	A key step to execute a change program is to define and prioritize the work that needs to be done. Identify the tasks, deliverables, and milestones that need to be achieved.
Teams	**Form teams & assign roles**
	Cross functional teams should be formed and roles and responsibilities with accountability should be assigned.
Execution	**Execute & monitor the plan.**
	Execute the plan and monitor progress so that goals are being met and that the program is on track. Use metrics to track progress, and adjust the plan as necessary.
Evaluation	**Evaluate the outcome.**
	On completion of the plan, it is important to evaluate the outcome, the success of the change & lessons learned.
Execute outcome	**Execute the change plan.**
	Execute the change plan including any necessary process changes, IT system updates, or other technical requirements.

3.2 Execution plan questions

General overview	Answering these questions will ensure that the execution plan is comprehensive and addresses all the necessary aspects.
Required actions	What are the actions that needed to implement the change?
Accountability	Who is responsible for each action with the completion date?
Status updates	How will the execution progress be tracked and measured?
Resources required	What resources (financial, personnel, etc.) are needed?
Comms & feedback	How will the change be communicated to stakeholders?
Risk management	What risks and potential obstacles have been identified?
Success metrics	How will the success of the execution be evaluated?
Sustainability	How will the change be sustained in the long term?
Integration	How will the change be integrated into the firm's culture?
Tech. requirements	How will the change be supported by the technology?
Support & training	What kind of support & training will be provided for staff?
Phases & roll out	How will the change be phased in and rolled out?

3.2 Execution plan components

General overview	Having these elements in the execution plan will ensure that the change can be implemented smoothly and effectively.
Specific objectives	Define clearly what is to be done &how it will be measured.
Detailed tasks and activities	Outline the stasks a that need to be completed to implement the change (timeline for when each task will be completed).
Responsibilities	Define the roles of all involved in the execution.
Resources	Identify the resources that are needed to implement the change (financial, staff, and technical resources).
Comms &stakeholder engagement	Outline how the change will be communicated to stakeholders and how feedback will be solicited?
Risk management	Identify potential risks and obstacles to the implementation and outline strategies for addressing them.
Evaluation and monitoring	Include methods for evaluating the success of the implementation and for monitoring progress.
Sustainability	Outline strategies for maintaining the change and integrating it into the organization's culture and processes.
Support	Identify the resources and support that will be provided to staff during the execution process & how it will be delivered.
Phasing and roll-out	Outline how the change will be phased in, and how it will be rolled out to different parts of the organization.

3.2 Execution plan best practices

General overview	By following these best practices, firms can increase the chances of a successful execution & reduce risk of failure.
Involve key stakeholders early	Involve key stakeholders in the development of the execution plan to ensure buy-in and support for the change.
Communicate clearly and often	Clearly communicate the plan to all stakeholders and provide regular updates on progress.
Assign clear roles and responsibilities	Clearly assign roles and responsibilities to all individuals and teams involved in the implementation.
Prioritize and focus on critical tasks	Prioritize and focus on the most critical tasks first to ensure that the change is implemented as quickly as possible.
Monitor progress and adjust as needed	Regularly monitor progress and adjust the plan as needed to ensure that the change is implemented successfully.
Consider potential risks and obstacles	Identify potential risks and obstacles to the implementation and develop strategies to address them.
Establish a governance structure	Establish a governance structure so that the execution stays on track &that decisions are made in a timely manner.
Provide training and support for employees	Provide training and support for staff to help them adjust to the change & ensure that they are able to perform their tasks.
Prepare for the unexpected	Be prepared for unexpected challenges and have contingency plans in place.
Evaluate and learn from the process	Evaluate the execution process, document what worked well and what didn't, and use this information for lessons learned.

3.2 Execution plan risks

General overview	By identifying and managing these risks, firms can increase the chance of a successful execution & reduce risk of failure.
Resistance to change	Staff may resist the change due to fear of the unknown, lack of understanding, or concerns about job security.
Lack of buy-in	Stakeholders may not fully support the change, which can make it difficult to implement.
Limited resources	The firm may not have the necessary financial, personnel, or technology resources to implement the change.
Inadequate communication	Poor comms can lead to confusion and frustration among staff which can negatively impact the implementation.
Lack of clear direction	Without a clear plan in place, it can be difficult to measure the success of the change and make adjustments as necessary.
Technical difficulties	Technical difficulties can cause delays and increase costs, making it more difficult to implement the change.
Dependence on external factors	The change may depend on external factors that are beyond the firm's control (changes in regulations or market conditions).
Limited support	Limited support from key stakeholders can make it more difficult to implement the change.
Inadequate training	Inadequate training can lead to staff not being able to perform their tasks effectively to negatively impact the execution.
Inaccurate forecasting and Budgeting	Inaccurate forecasting & budgeting can lead to unexpected costs to make it more difficult to implement the change.

3.2 Execution plan lessons learned

General overview	During the execute phase of a change program, the following lessons can be learned:
Communicate the plan clearly	Make sure that all stakeholders understand the plan and their roles in it. This helps to ensure that everyone is on the same page and working towards the same goals.
Be prepared for resistance	Change can be difficult for people, and they may resist it. Be prepared to address these concerns and provide support for those who are struggling with the changes.
Monitor progress closely	Regularly check in on progress and make adjustments as needed. This helps to ensure that the plan stays on track and that any issues are addressed in a timely manner.
Keep the end goal in mind	Remember why the change program is being implemented and stay focused on the ultimate goal. This can help to keep the team motivated and on task.
Be flexible	Be open to making changes to the plan as needed. Sometimes, things don't go as planned, and it's important to be able to adapt and make adjustments.
Celebrate successes	Recognize & reward the team for their hard work & results. This helps to build morale and maintain momentum.
Learn from failures	Failure is a part of any change program, and it's good to learn from it & use the lessons learned to improve future programs.

3.3 Resistance

The purpose of managing resistance to change in the execute phase of a change program is to mitigate the negative impact that resistance can have on the success of the change program. Resistance can come in many forms, such as lack of buy-in from employees, lack of communication, or lack of understanding of the change.

The goals of managing resistance to change include:

- Minimizing negative impact on the change program can be minimized, allowing the change to be implemented more effectively.
- Maintaining employee engagement helps to maintain employee engagement and commitment to the change program.
- Ensuring buy-in to ensure that all stakeholders are on board with the change and understand the reasons why it's being implemented.

The objectives of managing resistance to change include:

- Identifying and understanding resistance is key to managing it effectively.
- Communicating effectively the change program effectively can help to reduce resistance by ensuring that stakeholders understand the reasons for the change and their role in it.
- Providing support to employees who are struggling with the change can help to mitigate resistance and ensure that the change is implemented smoothly.
- Addressing concerns and providing solutions to problems that may arise can help to reduce resistance and ensure the success of the program.
- Continuously monitoring and evaluating resistance can help to identify issues early and take steps to address them.

3.3 Resistance workstream activities

Identification	**Understand the resistance.**
	Identify and understand the sources of resistance. This may involve conducting surveys, focus groups, or interviews to gather feedback and identify specific concerns.
Change benefits	**Communicate the benefits.**
	Clear communication is key to manage resistance to change. It is important to communicate the benefits of the change and how it will positively impact the firm and them (WIIFM).
Involvement	**Involve stakeholders in process**
	Involve stakeholders in the change process will build buy-in and reduce resistance. Provide training and education, and seeking input and feedback from stakeholders.
Transition support	**Support during transition.**
	Change can be difficult and stressful, and it is important to provide support to stakeholders during the transition. Provide resources, coaching, and mentoring as part of this support.
Issues	**Address & resolve any issues.**
	Address any issues that arise during the change process and resolve in a timely manner.
Resistance outcome	**Manage change resistance.**
	Identify and manage any resistance to the change from stakeholders.

3.3 Resistance questions

General overview	When managing resistance to change in the execute phase of a change program, some key questions to consider are:
The sources of resistance	**What are the sources of resistance?**
	Understanding the reasons behind resistance is key to managing it effectively. Identify any specific issues or concerns that employees may have with the change.
Effective comms	**How can the change be communicated more effectively?**
	Communicating the change program effectively can help to reduce resistance by ensuring that stakeholders understand the reasons for the change and their role in it.
Employee support	**What kind of support can be provided to employees?**
	Providing support to employees who are struggling with the change can help to mitigate resistance and ensure that the change is implemented smoothly.
Concerns to be addressed	**How can concerns be addressed?**
	Addressing concerns and providing solutions to problems that may arise can help to reduce resistance and ensure the success of the change program.

3.3 Resistance questions

Resistance metrics	**What are the metrics to measure resistance?**
	Resistance may not be a one-time event; it can come at different stages of the change journey. Identify the key metrics to measure resistance and track progress over time.
Staff engagement	**How to engage & involve staff in the change process?**
	Employees are more likely to resist a change that they do not understand or feel they have no control over. Engaging and involving employees in the change process can make them feel more invested in the change and reduce resistance.
Positive aspects of resistance	**How can we leverage the positive aspects of resistance?**
	Resistance is not always negative, it can be seen as a constructive feedback, it can be used to improve the change process and make it more effective.

3.3 Resistance plan components

General overview	There are several key elements to be included in a plan to manage resistance during the execution phase are.
Communication	Clearly communicate the rationale and benefits of the change to all stakeholders, and ensure that they understand how the change will affect them.
Involvement	Involve stakeholders in the planning & execution of the change to build buy-in and commitment to the change.
Training and support	Provide training and support to help stakeholders adapt to the new way of working, and address any of their concerns.
Monitoring and feedback	Monitor progress and provide regular feedback to stakeholders on the & make adjustments as necessary.
Resolve conflicts	Address any conflicts that may arise during the change process and find ways to resolve them.
Address resistance	Identify potential sources of resistance and develop strategies to address them as addressing concerns, providing incentives, or involving stakeholders in the change process.
Recognize and Reward	Recognize and reward those who have supported and embraced the change, to help reinforce the desired behaviours and build momentum for the change.

3.3 Resistance best practices

General overview	There are several best practices for managing resistance during the execution phase of a change program. It's also important to keep in mind that resistance is natural of any change & should be expected and managed accordingly.
Active listening	Listen actively to stakeholders' concerns and address them in a timely manner.
Transparency	Be transparent about the change process and keep stakeholders informed of progress.
Empowerment	Empower stakeholders by involving them in the change process & giving them a sense of ownership over the change.
Communication	Communicate the change effectively and frequently, using multiple channels to reach different stakeholders.
Address underlying concerns	Identify & address the underlying concerns and motivations of resistance, instead of addressing surface-level objections.
Address resistance early	Address resistance early on, before it becomes entrenched and harder to manage.
Be prepared	Anticipate resistance & have strategies in place to manage it.
Provide support	Provide support a to help stakeholders adapt to the change.
Be flexible on plan	Be flexible and willing to make adjustments as needed.
Lead by example	Lead by example for the desired behaviours and attitudes.

3.3 Resistance risks

General overview	There are several risks associated with managing resistance during the execution phase of a change program. It's important to keep in mind that resistance is not always negative, and could be the result of a lack of understanding or information, so it's important to identify and address the root cause of resistance.
Delayed implementation	Resistance can delay the implementation of the change, causing delays and additional costs.
Decreased buy-in	Resistance can decrease buy-in and commitment to the change, making it harder to achieve the desired outcomes.
Decreased employee morale	Resistance can decrease staff morale & engagement, leading to more absenteeism, turnover, a& decreased productivity.
Decreased customer satisfaction	Resistance can decrease customer satisfaction, leading to lost business and decreased revenue.
Legal risks	Resistance can lead to legal risks as discrimination claims, if certain parties are disproportionately affected by the change.
Reputation risks	Resistance can damage the firm's reputation if it is perceived as not being responsive to the needs of its stakeholders.
Conflicts	Resistance can lead to conflicts between stakeholders, which can be difficult to resolve and can further delay the change.
Misdiagnosis of resistance	Resistance can be misdiagnosed as lack of support for the change, which can lead to the wrong strategies being done.

3.3 Resistance lessons learned

General overview	t's also important to remember that change management is an ongoing process, and it's crucial to continuously evaluate the change program and adjust as needed.
Communication is key	Effective communication is crucial for managing resistance and building buy-in for the change.
Involvement matters	Involving stakeholders in the planning and execution of the change can build buy-in and commitment to the change.
Training and support are essential	Providing training & support can help stakeholders adapt to the new way of working & address any concerns they have.
Monitor and provide feedback	Monitoring progress and providing regular feedback can help to keep stakeholders informed & adjust as necessary.
Resistance is natural	Resistance is a natural part of any change process, and should be expected and managed accordingly.
Address underlying concerns	Ensuring to Identify and address the underlying concerns and motivations of resistance can be more effective.
Be prepared	Anticipating resistance and having strategies in place to manage it can help to mitigate its impact.
Be flexible	Be flexible to make adjustments to the plan as needed.
Lead by example	Lead by example to show the desired behaviours.
Continuously evaluate	Continuously evaluate and adjust the change plan as needed, and take into account the feedback and lessons learned during the execution phase.

3.4 Progress

The purpose of monitoring progress during the execution phase of a change program is to ensure that the program is on track to achieve its goals and objectives. The goals and objectives of the change program will vary depending on the specific program, but generally speaking, they will involve making changes to an organization or system in order to improve performance, efficiency, or effectiveness.

Monitoring progress allows for early identification of any issues or obstacles that may arise, and allows for corrective action to be taken in a timely manner to keep the program on track.

Additionally, monitoring progress also enables stakeholders to see the progress of the program, and provides an opportunity to gather feedback and make adjustments as needed to optimize the program's outcomes.

Not monitoring progress during the execution phase of a change program can have a number of negative impacts. Some of these include:

- Without monitoring progress, it can be difficult to identify when the program is falling behind schedule or experiencing other issues that may impede its progress. This can lead to delays in achieving the program's goals and objectives.
- Monitoring progress allows for early identification of areas where the program is not performing as well as expected, and provides an opportunity to make adjustments to improve performance. Without monitoring progress, these opportunities may be missed.

3.4 Progress workstream activities

Comms plan	**Establish a comms plan.**
	Create a comms plan to communicate progress for a change program to outline the key messages, audiences, and comms channels. This plan will be aligned with the program goals.
Updates	**Provide regular updates.**
	Provide regular updates on progress tailored to stakeholders specific needs (project status, milestones achieved, issues).
Comms channels	**Use multiple comms channels.**
	To reach a wide range of stakeholders, it use multiple communication channels (email, newsletters, intranet, video conferencing, and in-person meetings).
Success	**Communicate successes.**
	Communicating successes and celebrating achievements will build momentum and engagement. Highlight the positive impact of the change program & the progress made.
Feedback	**Gather feedback & address issues.**
	Gather feedback & address concerns important and use surveys, focus groups, or interviews to gather feedback and identify any issues or concerns that need to be addressed.
Progress outcome	**Communicate any progress.**
	Regularly communicate progress on the change program to stakeholders and address any concerns or issues that arise.

3.4 Progress questions

General overview	During the execution phase of a change program, it is important to monitor progress in order to ensure that the change is being implemented as planned and that desired outcomes are being achieved. Some key questions that can be used to monitor progress include:
Changes on target	Are the changes being executed on schedule & in budget?
Changes going to plan	Are the changes being implemented as planned and is the design of the change sound?
Stakeholders engaged	Are the stakeholders engaged and supportive of the change?
Desired outcomes being achieved	Are the desired outcomes being achieved and are there any unintended consequences?
Outstanding issues	Are there any issues that need to be addressed?
Adjustments required	Are any adjustments needed to the plan in order to ensure successful implementation?
Changes are being fully embedded	Has the change been fully embedded into the organization's systems, processes and culture?

3.4 Progress process steps

General overview	The process steps for monitoring progress during the execution phase of a change program may vary depending on the specific change program and organization, but generally, the process can include the following steps:
Establish a monitoring plan	Develop a plan that outlines the specific metrics, data sources, and methods that will be used to track progress.
Collect and analyse data	Gather data from various sources, such as project management software, surveys, and interviews, to measure progress against the established metrics.
Review progress	Review the data and analyse it to assess progress and identify any issues or concerns.
Communicate progress	Share progress updates with stakeholders, including the project team, management, and other affected parties.
Identify and address issues	Identify and address any issues that are impacting progress as lack of resources or resistance to the change.
Implement corrective actions	Develop and implement corrective actions to address identified issues & ensure the program stays on track.
Continuously monitor progress	Continuously monitor progress and repeat the above steps as necessary until the change program is fully implemented and embedded into the organization.
Evaluate the overall progress	After the change program is completed, evaluate the overall progress and outcome of the program, to identify any lessons learned and areas for future improvements.

3.4 Progress best practices

General overview	Best practices for monitoring progress during the execution phase of a change program can include the following:
Establish clear and measurable goals	Develop clear and measurable goals that align with the overall objectives of the change program. This will make it easier to track progress & see if the program is on track.
Use a variety of data sources	Gather data from multiple sources as PM software, surveys, and interviews, to get a more detailed view of progress.
Communicate regularly with stakeholders	Regularly communicate progress updates with stakeholders, including the project team, management, and other affected parties. This can help build buy-in & support for the program.
Address issues proactively	Identify and address any issues or roadblocks that are impacting progress as soon as they arise to prevent delays.
Continuously monitor progress	Continuously monitor progress throughout the execution phase, and adjust plans as necessary.
Foster transparency	Foster transparency and open comms so that everyone involved in the program is aware of the progress & status
Use a standard PM method	Use a standard PM method as PMBOK of PRINCE2 so that all aspects of the program are being tracked and monitored.
Evaluate the overall progress	After the change program is completed, evaluate the overall progress and outcome of the program, to identify any lessons learned and areas for future improvements.

3.4 Progress risks

General overview	Monitoring progress during the execution phase of a change program can help ensure that the change is being executed as planned and that desired outcomes are being achieved, but there are also potential risks that should be considered:
Distraction from the main goal	Constant monitoring can distract the team from their main goal and can make the team more focused on reporting progress than on delivering the change.
Resistance to change	Regular monitoring and reporting progress can increase the visibility of the change program and can make it more difficult to hide from stakeholders who may resist the change.
Over-reliance on data	Over-reliance on data can lead to a lack of understanding of the underlying causes of issues leading to superficial fixes.
Lack of ownership	Regular monitoring can create a perception that the change is being imposed from the top, rather than being owned by impacted staff, which can lead to resistance to change.
Unintended consequences	Regular monitoring can reveal unintended consequences of the change which can cause additional problems and make it difficult to maintain momentum.
Over-analysis	Monitoring progress can lead to over-analysing data, which can divert resources away from the program & slow progress.
Lack of flexibility	Regular monitoring can make it difficult to pivot or change course if the change program encounters unexpected issues.

3.4 Progress lessons learned

General overview	Some lessons that can be learned from monitoring progress during the execution phase of a change program include:
Clear and measurable goals	Having clear and measurable goals makes it easier to track progress and determine if the change program is on track.
The need for multiple data sources	Gathering data from multiple sources can give a more comprehensive view of progress.
The value of regular communication	Regularly communicating progress updates with stakeholders can help build buy-in and support for the change program.
Addressing issues proactively	Identifying and addressing issues as soon as they arise can help prevent delays and ensure the program stays on track.
Continuous monitoring	Continuously monitoring progress throughout the execution phase, and adjusting plans as necessary so that the change program is fully implemented and embedded into the firm.
Transparency and open communication	Transparency and open communication can help everyone involved in the change program to be aware of the progress and the status of the program.
The value of using a standard framework	Using a standard framework can ensure that all aspects of the change program are being tracked and monitored.
Evaluating the overall progress	After the change program is completed, evaluating the overall progress and outcome of the program can help identify any lessons learned and areas for future improvements.

3.5 Embedding

The purpose of embedding during the execution phase of a change program is to ensure that the changes made during the program are sustained and become a part of the organization's culture. The goals and objectives of embedding during this phase include:

- Ensuring that the changes made during the program are fully understood and adopted by all staff.
- Making sure that the changes are integrated into the organization's systems, processes, and policies.
- Building the necessary skills and capabilities within the organization to support and maintain the changes.
- Creating a culture of continuous improvement that supports ongoing change and adaptability.
- Monitoring and measuring the progress and impact of the changes to ensure they are delivering the desired results.

Not embedding during the execution phase of a change program can lead to a number of negative impacts, including:

- If changes are not fully understood or adopted by employees, it can lead to resistance and reluctance to implement them.
- Without embedding, the changes may not be fully integrated into the organization's systems, processes and policies, leading employees to revert back to old ways of working.
- The changes may not be sustained over time and may not deliver the desired results.
- The resources invested in the change program, such as time, money and effort may be wasted.
- Without a culture of continuous improvement, an organization may struggle to adapt to new challenges and opportunities.

3.5 Embedding workstream activities

Accountability	**Establish clear accountability.**
	Establish clear accountability and ownership for the change. Assign roles and responsibilities, and holding individuals and teams accountable for achieving specific goals & objectives.
Incorporation	**Incorporate the change into BAU.**
	Incorporate the change into day-to-day operations so it becomes a permanent part of the firm's culture & processes. Incorporate change into performance & training programs.
Celebration	**Celebrate the change.**
	Continuous communication and celebration of the change is key to keep the momentum of the change program going so that the change is fully understood and embraced by the firm.
Monitoring	**Monitor progress & adjust as need.**
	Continuously monitor progress and adjust the change program as needed so that the change is fully embedded.
Capability	**Build in-house capability.**
	Build in-house capability to embed the change. Provide training opportunities & encourage staff to take ownership of the change and develop their skills & knowledge.
Embed change	**Embed the change.**
	Make the change part of the firm's business as usual, and that it is integrated into the firm's culture and processes.

3.5 Embedding questions

General overview	During the execution phase of a change program, it is key to ask the following questions about embedding the change:
Change comms approach	How will the change be communicated and reinforced to ensure it is fully understood and adopted by all stakeholders?
Change integration process	How will the change be integrated into daily processes and systems to ensure it becomes a permanent part of the organization's culture and operations?
Monitoring & evaluation of change	How will the change be monitored and evaluated so it is having its goals & making a positive impact on the firm?
Feedback process & improvement inputs	How will feedback be collected and acted upon to make adjustments and improvements to the change as needed?
Sustainable change over time	How will the change be sustained over time to ensure it does not revert back to previous ways of doing things?
Link between change & overall strategy	How will the change be linked with the overall strategy and objectives of the organization?

3.5 Embedding plan components

General overview	An embedding plan is a crucial component of the execution phase of a change program, as it outlines the steps and strategies for ensuring the change becomes a permanent part of the organization's culture and operations. Some core elements of an embedding plan include:
Communication and reinforcement	A clear and consistent communication strategy that outlines how the change will be communicated and reinforced to all stakeholders (staff, customers, and other key groups).
Integration into daily processes & systems	A plan for how the change will be integrated into the firms systems and processes & required training and support.
Monitoring and evaluation	A system for monitoring and evaluating the progress and impact of the change, including KPIs and metrics.
Feedback and adjustment to plan	A process for collecting and acting upon feedback from stakeholders to make adjustments and improvements.
Sustainability	Strategies for ensuring the change is sustained over time, including reinforcement and training programs, and processes to monitor and evaluate the change.
Alignment with overall strategy	A clear alignment with the overall strategy and objectives of the organization to ensure the change is embedded in the organization's culture and future direction.
Governance and Ownership	A plan for assigning ownership and governance of the change and embedding it within the organization.
Resources	Identifying and allocating the resources to implement the embedding plan (training, technology and human resources).

3.5 Embedding best practices

General overview	Embedding a change as part of the execution phase in a change program is crucial for ensuring the change becomes a permanent part of the organization's culture and operations.
Involve stakeholders in the process	Involving stakeholders in the change process, such as employees, customers, and other key groups, can help to build buy-in so the change is fully understood and adopted.
Communicate clearly and consistently	Communicating the change clearly and consistently, including the reasons for the change, the benefits, and the expected outcomes, can help to build support and understanding.
Train and support employees	Providing training and support to employees can help them to understand the change, develop the necessary skills and knowledge, and feel confident in implementing the change.
Integrate the change into processes	Integrating the change into the firm's systems and processes so it becomes a permanent part of the firm's operations.
Monitor and evaluate progress	Regularly monitoring and evaluating the progress and the change impact c to identify any issues &make adjustments.
Reinforce and sustain the change	Continuously reinforcing and sustaining the change can help to ensure it is not forgotten or abandoned.
Align with overall strategy	Align the change with the overall strategy and objectives of the firm so the change is embedded in the 's culture.
Govern and assign ownership	Assign ownership and governance of the change to ensure it is embedded within the firm and supported by the leadership.
Continuously learn and improve	Continuously learning & improving from feedback and monitoring the change progress to make any adjustments.

3.5 Embedding risks

General overview	Embedding a change as part of the execution phase in a change program is a crucial step in ensuring the change becomes a permanent part of the organization's operations.
Resistance to change	Employees and other stakeholders may resist the change due to a lack of understanding or fear of the unknown.
Inadequate comms and reinforcement	Poor comms and a lack of reinforcement can lead to confusion about the change, which can result in low adoption.
Lack of training and support	Without proper training & support, staff may struggle to know how to use the new systems or processes.
Integrating the change into daily processes	Integrating the change into daily processes and systems can be a complex, time-consuming task for resources.
Limited buy-in from leadership	Without buy-in and support from leadership, it can be difficult to embed the change within the firm's culture and operations.
Limited resources	Insufficient resources such as time, budget or skill set may impact the ability to implement the embedding plan effectively
Sustainability	Without proper reinforcement, the change may not be sustained over time and the firm may revert back old ways.
Lack of alignment with overall strategy	Not aligning the change with the overall strategy and objectives of the organization can lead to the change not being embedded in the firm's culture and future direction.
Governance and ownership	Without proper governance and ownership of the change, it may not be embedded within the organization and may lack support from leadership.

3.5 Embedding lessons learned

General overview	Embedding a change as part of the execution phase in a change program can be a complex and challenging process.
Involve stakeholders in the change process	Involving stakeholders in the change process helps to build buy-in so the change is fully understood and adopted.
The need for clear and consistent comms	Clear and consistent comms is crucial for building support &understanding for the change & for addressing any issues
The value of training and support	Providing training and support to staff can help them to understand the change, & develop the necessary skills .
Integrate the change into daily processes	Integrating the change into the firm's systems and processes can be a complex & time-consuming task for staff.
Monitoring and evaluating progress	Regularly monitoring & evaluating the progress & the change impact helps to identify any issues & adjust as needed.
Reinforcement and sustainability	Continuously reinforcing and sustaining the change can help to ensure it is not forgotten or abandoned.
Alignment with overall strategy	Align the change with the overall strategy and objectives of the firm so the change is embedded in the firm's culture.
Governance and ownership	Assign ownership and governance of the change to ensure it is embedded within the firm and supported by the leadership.
Continuous learning and improvement	Continuously learning and improving from feedback and monitoring the progress & to make adjustments as needed.
The need for adequate resources	Identifying and allocating the necessary resources to execute the embedding plan (training, technology and people).

CORRECTION DOES MUCH, BUT ENCOURAGEMENT DOES MORE.

Johann Wolfgang von Goethe

4.0 Monitoring

The primary goal of the monitoring and evaluation phase in a change management program is to measure the success of the changes implemented and evaluate the effectiveness of the change management program. This includes monitoring the progress of the implementation, measuring the performance of the organization against the objectives set in the planning phase, and assessing the impact of the changes on the stakeholders. The monitoring and evaluation phase also includes identifying any issues or challenges that arise during implementation and making necessary adjustments to the change management plan. The goal of this phase is to ensure that the changes have been successful in achieving the intended outcome, and to identify any areas for improvement for future change management initiatives.

What are the 5 key components and associated activities for the monitoring and evaluation phase for a change management program?

1. Measuring progress is the monitoring of progress against the goals and milestones established during the planning phase.
2. Evaluating outcomes involves evaluating the outcomes of the change program, including any benefits realised.
3. Identifying issues is the identifying of any issues that arise during the implementation of the change program and taking appropriate action to address them.
4. Communicating the results of the change program to stakeholders and using this feedback to make any necessary adjustments.
5. Continual improvement involves using the results of the monitoring and evaluation phase to identify opportunities for continual improvement of the change program and adjust as needed

4.0 Monitoring Plan Linkages

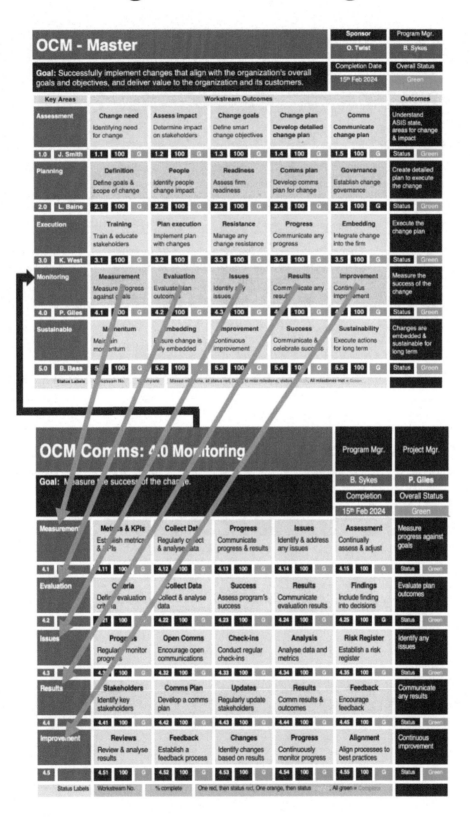

4.0 Monitoring Workstream Plan

OCM Comms: 4.0 Monitoring				Program Mgr.	Project Mgr.
Goal: Measure the success of the change.				B. Sykes	**P. Giles**
				Completion	Overall Status
				15th Feb 2024	Green

Measurement	**Metrics & KPIs** Establish metrics & KPIs	**Collect Data** Regularly collect & analyse data	**Progress** Communicate progress & results	**Issues** Identify & address any issues	**Assessment** Continually assess & adjust	Measure progress against goals
4.1	4.11 100 G	4.12 100 G	4.13 100 G	4.14 100 G	4.15 100 G	Status Green
Evaluation	**Criteria** Define evaluation criteria	**Collect Data** Collect & analyse data	**Success** Assess program's success	**Results** Communicate evaluation results	**Findings** Include finding into decisions	Evaluate plan outcomes
4.2	4.21 100 G	4.22 100 G	4.23 100 G	4.24 100 G	4.25 100 G	Status Green
Issues	**Progress** Regularly monitor progress	**Open Comms** Encourage open communications	**Check-ins** Conduct regular check-ins	**Analysis** Analyse data and metrics	**Risk Register** Establish a risk register	Identify any issues
4.3	4.31 100 G	4.32 100 G	4.33 100 G	4.34 100 G	4.35 100 G	Status Green
Results	**Stakeholders** Identify key stakeholders	**Comms Plan** Develop a comms plan	**Updates** Regularly update stakeholders	**Results** Comm results & outcomes	**Feedback** Encourage feedback	Communicate any results
4.4	4.41 100 G	4.42 100 G	4.43 100 G	4.44 100 G	4.45 100 G	Status Green
Improvement	**Reviews** Review & analyse results	**Feedback** Establish a feedback process	**Changes** Identify changes based on results	**Progress** Continuously monitor progress	**Alignment** Align processes to best practices	Continuous improvement
4.5	4.51 100 G	4.52 100 G	4.53 100 G	4.54 100 G	4.55 100 G	Status Green
Status Labels	Workstream No.	% complete	One red, then status red, One orange, then status		All green = Complete	

4.1 Measurement

The purpose of measurement in the monitoring phase of a strategic organization change management program is to assess the progress and effectiveness of the change initiative, and determine if the change is achieving the desired outcomes.

The objectives of measurement in the monitoring phase typically include:

- Measuring and tracking progress against the established goals and objectives of the change initiative
- Identifying any barriers or obstacles that may be impeding progress
- Assessing the effectiveness of the change management strategies and tactics being used
- Gathering feedback from stakeholders to identify areas for improvement
- Communicating progress and results to key stakeholders and leadership

The goals of measurement in the monitoring phase include:

- Establishing a baseline to measure progress
- Identifying areas of improvement and progress
- Identifying and tracking key performance indicators (KPIs)
- Gathering data to support decisions about future changes
- Continuously monitoring progress to ensure the change initiative is on track and achieving the desired outcomes.

Overall, the measurement in the monitoring phase is a vital aspect that enables leaders to evaluate the effectiveness of their change management strategies, and make any necessary adjustments to ensure the success of the change initiative.

4.1 Measurement workstream activities

Metrics & KPIs	Establish metrics & KPIs.
	Establishing metrics and key performance indicators (KPIs) to measure progress against objectives.
Collect data	Regularly collect & analyse data.
	Regularly collect and analyse data on performance against these metrics and KPIs.
Progress	Communicate progress & results.
	Communicate progress and results to stakeholders (leaders and team members).
Issues	Identify & address any issues.
	Identify and addressing any issues or challenges that arise during the program.
Assessment	Continually assess & adjust.
	Continuously assess and adjust the program as needed to ensure it stays on track to meet its objectives.
Measurement outcome	Measure progress against goals.
	Monitor progress against the objectives and milestones established during the planning phase.

4.1 Measurement questions

General overview	It is important to note that questions may vary depending on the specifics of the program and the goals and objectives that have been established. The key is to focus on the most important aspects of the program and measure progress accordingly. Key questions for measurement in the monitoring phase of a change program may include:
On track with goals	Are we on track to achieve our goals and objectives?
Issues hurting goals	Are there any issues preventing us from achieving our goals?
Effective strategies	Are the strategies that we are using effective?
Program impact on organisation	What is the impact of the program on key stakeholders and the organization as a whole?
Stakeholder feedback	What feedback do stakeholders have about the program?
Success identification	Have any successes, good practices or opportunities for improvement been identified?
Improvement ideas	How can we improve the program moving forward?
Best way to comm program results	How can we communicate the program results to stakeholders involved in the change program?
Planning phase targets or milestones	Are the specific targets or milestones established in the planning phase been met?
Key performance indicators (KPIs)	Are the key performance indicators (KPIs) that were established in the planning phase being achieved?

4.1 Measurement plan

General overview	A measurement plan in the monitoring phase of a change program typically includes the following key elements:
Goals and objectives	Clearly define the goals and objectives of the program, as well as the specific targets that need to be achieved.
Key performance indicators (KPIs)	Identify the specific indicators that will be used to track progress towards the program's goals and objectives
Data collection methods	Specify how data will be collected, including the type of data that will be collected and the tools that will be used.
Data analysis methods	State how data will be analysed, including the methods that will be used to process and interpret the data.
Reporting and communication	Define how data will be reported and communicated to stakeholders, including the frequency & format of reports.
Evaluation criteria	Define the evaluation criteria which will be used to assess the effectiveness of the program's interventions or strategies.
Data governance	Define the data governance & data management protocols to be used so the accuracy, completeness of the data collected.
Resources	Identify the resources that will be required to implement the plan, including personnel, equipment, and budget.
Timeline	Determine a timeline for data collection, analysis, and reporting, including regular intervals and milestones.

4.1 Measurement workstream best practices

General overview	There are several best practices for measurement during the monitoring phase of a change program:
Establish clear and measurable goals	Identify specific, measurable objectives for the change program to be used to track progress & determine success.
Use appropriate metrics	Select metrics that are relevant to the goals of the change program and that can be easily collected and analysed.
Regularly collect and analyse data	Regularly collect data on the metrics identified and analyse it to track progress and identify areas for improvement.
Communicate results	Share the results of the monitoring and measurement efforts with stakeholders to keep them informed of progress and to gain buy-in for any necessary adjustments to the program.
Continuously improve	Use the information gathered during monitoring to identify areas for improvement and make adjustments as needed.
Different methods	Use different methodologies to measure the change.
Feedback loop	Create a feedback loop to get insights from the people who are impacted by the change.

44.1 Measurement workstream risks

General overview	There are several risks associated with measurement during the monitoring phase of a change program:
Inaccurate data	Incorrect data collection or analysis can lead to inaccurate results and a false understanding of progress.
Lack of buy-in	If stakeholders do not understand or agree with the metrics being used, they may not support the change program or take ownership of their role in its success.
Limited scope	Measuring only certain aspects of the change program can lead to an incomplete understanding of progress & success.
Unforeseen challenges	The change program may encounter unforeseen challenges that can't be captured by the metrics that were initially set.
Limited resources	Collecting and analysing data can be time-consuming and resource-intensive, which may be a limitation in the program.
Biased data	It is important to be aware of the biases that might be affecting the measurement, if the data is self-reported.
Limited understanding of the change	If the change program has not been well-communicated to the team responsible for measurement, they may not have the needed understanding to accurately measure progress.

4.1 Measurement workstream lessons

General overview	There are several key lessons that can be learned from measurement during the monitoring phase of a program:
Establish clear and measurable goals	Identify specific, measurable goals for the change program that can be used to track progress and determine success.
Use appropriate metrics	Select metrics that are relevant to the goals of the change program and that can be easily collected and analysed.
Regularly collect and analyse data	Regularly collect data on the metrics identified and analyse it to track progress and identify areas for improvement.
Communicate results	Share the results of the monitoring and measurement efforts with key stakeholders to keep them informed of progress.
Continuously improve	Use the information gathered during monitoring to identify areas for improvement and make adjustments as needed.
The importance of measurement	Communicate the importance of measurement & the role it plays in the success of the change program stakeholders.
Team for metrics understands program	Ensure that the team responsible for measurement understands the change program and the metrics being used.
Be prepared to adapt	Be prepared to adapt the metrics used to measure progress as the program evolves & unforeseen challenges arise.
Use different methodologies	Use different methodologies and sources to validate the results and to triangulate the data.
Culture of continuous improvement	Create a culture of continuous improvement by using the data and feedback to continuously adjust the change program.

4.2 Evaluation

The purpose of evaluation in the monitoring phase of a change program is to assess the progress of the program in achieving its goals and objectives. The goals and objectives of evaluation during this phase may include:

- Measuring the progress of the program against the set targets.

- Identifying any issues or challenges that have arisen and addressing them in a timely manner.

- Assessing the impact of the program on stakeholders.

- Identifying areas for improvement and making adjustments to the program as necessary.

- Providing feedback to program managers and staff to inform decision-making and future planning.

Poor evaluation in the monitoring phase of a change program can have several negative impacts, including:

- Without adequate evaluation, it may be difficult to determine whether the program is making progress towards its goals, making it difficult to identify areas that need improvement.

- Poor evaluation can result in missed opportunities for identifying and addressing issues and challenges, which can lead to suboptimal program outcomes.
- Without adequate evaluation, it may be difficult to demonstrate the impact of the program to stakeholders, including funders and partners. This can make it more difficult to secure future funding and support.

4.2 Evaluation workstream activities

Criteria	**Define evaluation criteria.** Define and agree on the evaluation criteria and methods to measure the outcomes of the change program.
Collect data	**Collect and analyse data.** Collect and analyse data on the program outcomes using the established evaluation criteria.
Success	**Assess the program's success.** Assess the program's success in achieving its objectives and identify areas for improvement.
Results	**Communicate evaluation results.** Communicate the evaluation results to key stakeholders, including leadership and team members.
Findings	**Include findings into decisions.** Incorporate the evaluation findings into future planning and decision-making for the change program.
Evaluation outcome	**Evaluate plan outcomes.** Evaluate the outcomes of the change program and any improvements or benefits realized.

4.2 Evaluation questions

General overview	Evaluation in the monitoring phase of a change program typically involves answering a variety of questions in order to assess progress and effectiveness. These questions may be used as a starting point, but it is important to tailor the evaluation process to the specific program, its goals and objectives, and the needs of the stakeholders.
On track to meet goals	Are we on track to achieve our goals and objectives?
Any issues to resolve	Are there any issues that have arisen need to be addressed?
Impact of program	What impact is the program having on stakeholders?
Improvement areas	Are there any areas of the program that need improvement?
Program staff support	How best to support program staff achieving program goals?
Show program impact	How to demonstrate the program impact to stakeholders?
Strategies & tactics	Are the strategies and tactics being used effective?
Resource utilisation	Are the resources being used efficiently?
Any changes needed	Are there any changes needed in the program design?
Unintended outcomes	Are there any unintended outcomes & steps to avoid them?
Expected results	Are the expected results on track to be achieved on time?
Program in budget	Are the expected results being achieved within budget?

4.2 Evaluation plan components

General overview	Overall, a well-designed evaluation plan in the monitoring phase of a change program will help ensure that the program is on track to achieve its goals and objectives, and that any necessary adjustments are made to keep it on track.
Evaluation questions	These specific questions that the evaluation will seek to answer in order to assess progress of the program.
Data collection methods	The methods that will be used to gather data and information to answer the evaluation questions (surveys, interviews).
Data analysis plan	Outline how the data will be analysed to answer the evaluation questions (details on statistical methods, data visualization techniques, and data management procedures).
Performance indicators	These are specific, measurable and relevant data points that will be used to track the progress of the program.
Timelines and milestones	The specific dates and points in time when data collection and analysis will take place & when results will be reported.
Reporting a dissemination plan	Outline how the results of the evaluation will be shared with stakeholders (program staff, managers, funders a& partners).
Evaluation team	Include the staff who will be responsible for carrying out the evaluation (leader, data collectors, analysts, report writers).
Budget and resource allocation	Outlines the financial and human resources required to carry out the evaluation.

4.2 Evaluation best practices

General overview	Overall, best practices for an evaluation plan in the monitoring phase of a change program focus on using multiple data collection methods, regular reporting and dissemination, involving stakeholders, being flexible and using technology, and continuous improvement in order to achieve the program's goals and objectives.
Clearly defined goals and objectives:	The evaluation plan should be aligned with the program goals & should be used to measure progress and effectiveness.
Use of multiple data collection methods	Using multiple methods such as surveys, interviews, focus groups, and program data analysis will provide a more comprehensive understanding of the program's progress.
Use of performance indicators	The plan should include specific, measurable and relevant performance indicators that can be used to track progress and determine whether the program is achieving its goals.
Regular reporting and dissemination	Incorporate regular reporting and dissemination of results to stakeholders (program staff, managers, funders and partners) so that they can be informed and engaged in the process.

4.2 Evaluation best practices

Flexibility	The plan should be flexible and allow for adjustments as needed, to adapt to the changing needs of the program.
Involvement of stakeholders	Involve the participation of stakeholders, including program staff, managers, funders, and partners, in order to gain their perspectives, insights and buy-in.
Use of technology	Take advantage of technology, like data visualization tools to help with data analysis, reporting and sharing results.
Continuous improvement	The evaluation plan should be used to identify areas for improvement and make program adjustments as need, to achieve its goals and objectives.
Use of a logic model	A logic model can be used to map out the program's goals, objectives, inputs, activities, outputs and outcomes, which can be used as a framework for the evaluation plan.

4.2 Evaluation risks

General overview	There are several risks associated with evaluation in the monitoring phase of a change program, including:
Limited data	The data collected during the monitoring phase may be insufficient to accurately evaluate the program effectiveness.
Bias	The evaluation process may be influenced by personal unobjective biases, leading to inaccurate conclusions.
Misinterpretation of data	The data collected may be misinterpreted or misunderstood, leading to inaccurate conclusions about the change program.
Lack of buy-in	If stakeholders are not invested in the change program, they may be less likely to participate in the evaluation process or provide honest feedback.
Resistance to change	The evaluation process may reveal resistance to the change program, which can make it more difficult to implement it.
Limited resources	The evaluation process may be hampered by lack of time and/or budget, leading to less accurate results.
Misaligned goals	The evaluation process may reveal that the goals of the change program are not aligned with the needs of the organization or its stakeholders.

4.2 Evaluation lessons learned

General overview	There are several key lessons that can be learned from the evaluation of the monitoring phase of a program, including:
Clear and measurable goals	Having clear and measurable goals for the change program can make it easier to evaluate its progress and effectiveness.
The need for accurate and reliable data	Accurate and reliable data is essential for evaluating the change program, and it's important to ensure that the data collection process is unbiased and objective.
The importance of stakeholder buy-in	Stakeholder buy-in is crucial for the success of a change program, and the evaluation process should involve input from all relevant stakeholders.
Ongoing monitoring and evaluation	Monitoring and evaluating the change program on an ongoing basis is necessary to ensure that it stays on track and to make any necessary adjustments
Address resistance to change	Resistance to change is a common challenge, and the evaluation process should identify any areas of resistance and develop strategies to address them.
The importance of aligning goals	The evaluation process should ensure that the goals of the change program are aligned with the needs and priorities of the organization and its stakeholders.
Continuous improvement	The evaluation process should be used as an opportunity for continuous improvement and make adjustments as needed

4.3 Issues

During the monitoring phase of a change program, several issues may arise, including:

- Some individuals or groups within the organization may be resistant to the changes being implemented, which can impede progress.
- Poor communication can lead to confusion and misunderstandings about the change program and its objectives.
- The change program may require additional resources (financial, personnel, or technological) that are not readily available.
- Without proper training, employees may struggle to adapt to the new processes or systems being implemented.
- It can be difficult to measure the progress and effectiveness of the change program, which makes it challenging to identify areas for improvement.

- Ensuring that the changes are sustainable in the long-term and ensuring that the progress made is not lost after the program is complete.
- If key stakeholders are not on board with the change program, it may be difficult to secure the support and resources needed to implement the changes successfully.

If issues are not effectively dealt with during the monitoring phase of a change program, it can lead to a number of negative consequences, including:

- When key issues are not addressed, the change program may fail to achieve its objectives or may fail altogether.
- Issues that are allowed to linger, they can slow down on the change program, causing momentum to be lost.
- When issues are not dealt with in a timely manner, they can lead to increased resistance to change among employees and other stakeholders.
- Ignoring issues can lead to increased costs from wasted resources and the need to address problems later on.

4.3 Issues workstream activities

Progress	**Regularly monitor progress.**
	Regularly monitor progress against the program's objectives and metrics.
Open comms	**Encourage open communications.**
	Encourage open communication among team members and stakeholders to identify any issues or concerns.
Check-ins	**Conduct regular check-ins.**
	Conduct regular check-ins and reviews to assess the program's progress and identify any potential issues.
Analysis	**Analyse data and metrics.**
	Analyse data and performance metrics to detect any unexpected patterns or deviations from the plan.
Risk register	**Establish a risk register.**
	Establish a system to report and track issue in a risk register so that they are identified and addressed in a timely manner.
Issues outcome	**Identify any issues.**
	Identify any issues that arise during the execution of the change program and taking action to address them.

4.3 Issues questions

General overview	When dealing with issues during the monitoring phase of a change program, it's important to ask several key questions to help identify the root cause of the problem and determine the most effective course of action. By asking these questions, firms can better understand the nature of the issues they are facing and develop effective solutions that address the root causes of the problem.
The problem	What specific problem or challenge is being encountered?
Cause of problem	What is the cause of the issue (a lack of resources, insufficient training, poor comms, resistance to change)?
The impact on the change program	How is the issue impacting the change program (the consequences of the issue, and its effect on progress)?
Impacted stakeholders	Who is affected by the issue (owner of the issue, and the staff be impacted by any potential solutions)?
Potential solutions and actions	What are the potential solutions to the issue (the actions to be taken to address the problem, and the resources need)?
Solution success metrics	How can we measure the effectiveness of the solution (the metrics to be used to measure the progress of the solution)?
Sustainable solutions	How to make sure that the solutions are sustainable(so that the progress made is not lost after the program is complete)?
Stakeholder support for solution	How to ensure that the key stakeholders are on board with the solutions so that the support and resources needed to implement the changes successfully are secured?

4.3 Issues process steps

General overview	Several process steps that organizations can follow to help ensure that problems are effectively addressed and resolved. By following these steps, organizations can more effectively identify, analyse, and address issues that arise during the monitoring phase of a change program, helping to ensure that the change program is successful.
Identification	Identify the specific issues that are impacting the change program. This can involve conducting interviews, surveys, or focus groups with employees and stakeholders to gather information about the problems they are encountering.
Analysis	Analyse the data collected to understand the root cause of the issues. This may involve identifying patterns, trends, or common themes among the issues identified.
Planning	Develop a plan to address the issues identified. This may involve identifying potential solutions, determining the resources required, and assigning responsibilities to people.
Implementation	Implement the solutions identified in the planning stage. This may involve providing more training, convey the changes to staff, or making changes to processes or systems.

4.3 Issues process steps

Evaluation	Evaluate the effectiveness of the solutions implemented. This may involve tracking progress using metrics and indicators, and collecting feedback from employees and stakeholders.
Adjusting	Based on the evaluation, make adjustments to the solutions as needed. This may involve continuing to refine the solutions over time, or even developing new solutions if the initial ones are not working as expected.
Sustainability	Develop a plan to ensure that the changes are sustainable in the long-term. This may involve creating a system of checks and balances, or assigning a specific team or individual to be responsible for maintaining the changes.
Communication	Keep key stakeholders informed of the progress and any issues that arise. This will help to ensure that all are aware of what is happening & any potential risks that might arise.

4.3 Issues best practices

General overview	When dealing with issues during the monitoring phase of a change program, there are several best practices that firms can follow so that problems are addressed & resolved. By following these best practices, organizations can more effectively identify, analyse, and address issues that arise during the monitoring phase of a change program, helping to ensure that the change program is successful.
Communication	Establish clear and open lines of communication so that all stakeholders are aware of the issues and any solutions.
Involvement	Encourage the involvement of employees and stakeholders in the process of identifying, analysing and addressing issues. This will help to build buy-in and ownership of the solution among those who will be impacted.
Flexibility	Be prepared to adapt and adjust solutions as needed. The change process is dynamic and issues may arise that require a different approach.
Prioritization	Prioritize issues based on their impact on the change program and the organization. This will help to ensure that the most critical problems are addressed first.

4.3 Issues best practices

Root Cause Analysis	Use root cause analysis techniques to identify the underlying causes of issues, rather than just treating the symptoms.
Collaboration	Collaborate with other teams and departments within the organization to share knowledge and resources.
Training	Provide training and support to help employees and stakeholders adapt to the changes.
Measurement	Establish a system for measuring the progress and effectiveness of the solutions, and use this information to make adjustments as needed
Sustainability	Develop a plan for ensuring that the changes are sustainable in the long-term.
Follow-up	Follow-up on the issues that have been resolved, to ensure that the solution is working as intended.

4.3 Issues risks

General overview	When dealing with issues during the monitoring phase of a program, there are several risks that firms may encounter. By identifying and mitigating these risks, firms can more deal better with issues that arise during the monitoring phase of a change program, increasing the chances of success.
Resistance to change	Stakeholders may be resistant to the changes being made, which can impede progress a& make it difficult to fix issues.
Lack of buy-in	Key stakeholders may not be on board with the change program, which can make it difficult to secure the support and resources needed to implement the changes.
Inadequate resources	The change program may require additional resources (financial, personnel, or technological) that are not available.
Insufficient training	Without proper training, employees may struggle to adapt to the new processes or systems being implemented.
Damage to reputation	If the change program is perceived as failing or being mismanaged, it can damage the reputation of the firm.
Decrease in employee morale	If the issues are not addressed effectively, employees may become disengaged and demotivated, which can lead to decreased productivity and increased turnover.
Inability to achieve desired outcomes	Without addressing the issues that arise during the monitoring phase, it may be difficult to achieve the desired outcomes and reach the objectives of the change program.
Cost	Ignoring issues or addressing them in a wrong way can lead to increased costs, such as wasted resources, delays, and the need to address problems later on.

4.3 Issues lessons learned

Clear comms channels	Clear comms channels for timely reporting & issue resolution.
Assigning ownership of issues	Identifying and assigning ownership of issues so that issues are owned and followed up on its resolution.
Looking for issue patterns	Tracking and documenting issues for the identification of patterns, helps to prevent the same issues from recurring.
Regular reviews & updates on issues	Regularly reviewing and updating the issue resolution process so that the process remains effective and efficient.
Encourage feedback on solutions	Encouraging feedback and continuous improvement for the identification & execution of solutions.
Regular updates on progress	Regularly reviewing and reporting on progress for the identification of any issues that may be hindering progress and helps to ensure that the change program stays on track.
A culture of accountability	Building a culture of accountability to ensure that everyone involved in the change program takes ownership of their role and is committed to its success.

4.4 Results

The purpose of the results in the monitoring phase of a change program is to evaluate the effectiveness and progress of the change implementation.

This includes assessing whether the change has met its intended goals and objectives, identifying any issues or obstacles that have arisen, and determining if any adjustments or further actions are needed to ensure the success of the change program.

The results from the monitoring phase can also be used to make informed decisions about the future direction of the change program.

Not evaluating results as part of the monitoring phase for a change program can have several negative impacts, including:

- Without monitoring and evaluating results, it may be difficult to determine if the change program is making progress towards its intended goals. This can lead to wasted resources and a lack of progress.

- Without monitoring and evaluating results, it may be difficult to identify and address issues or obstacles that arise during the change program. This can lead to inefficiencies in the change process and prolong the time required to implement the change.

- It may be difficult to hold individuals or teams accountable for the progress and success of the program.

- Making informed decisions may be difficult about the future direction of the change program. This can make it difficult to adapt to changing circumstances and respond to new challenges or opportunities.

- Maintaining the support and buy-in of stakeholders may be difficult in the change program. Stakeholders may become disengaged if they don't see progress or results from the program.

4.4 Results workstream activities

Stakeholders	**Identify key stakeholders.**
	Identify key stakeholders and determining the appropriate communication channels for each group.
Comms plan	**Develop a comms plan.**
	Develop a communication plan that outlines the message, audience, and timing for each communication.
Updates	**Regularly update stakeholders.**
	Regularly update stakeholders on the progress of the program and any significant developments.
Results	**Communicate results & outcomes.**
	Communicate results & outcomes using clear and concise language & visual aids for information easy to understand.
Feedback	**Encourage feedback.**
	Encourage feedback and address any questions or concerns from stakeholders in a timely and transparent manner.
Results outcome.	**Communicate the results.**
	Communicate the results of the change program to stakeholders & use this feedback to make any adjustments.

4.4 Results questions

General overview	Answering these questions can help determine the effectiveness and progress of the change program, identify any issues or obstacles that have arisen, and make informed decisions about the future direction of the change program.
Program goals & objectives	What are the intended goals and objectives of the change program, and how well are they being met?
Issues & obstacles that have arisen	What issues or obstacles have arisen during the change program, and how are they being addressed?
Current progress against goals	What progress has been made towards the intended goals and objectives of the change program?
Any program adjustments needed	Are there any adjustments or further actions needed to ensure the success of the change program?
Results aligned with expectations	Are the results of the program in line with the expectations and predictions made during the planning phase?
KPIs being met	Are the key performance indicators (KPIs) established during the planning phase being met?
Unintended consequences	Have any unintended consequences of the change program been identified and how they are being addressed?
Staff satisfaction	Are the stakeholders satisfied with the progress and results?
Lessons learned	Are there any lessons learned from the monitoring phase that can be applied to future change programs?
Next steps	Based on the results, what is the next step for the program?

4.4 Results process components

General overview	It's important to note that the monitoring process should be designed to be agile, responsive and allow for flexibility to adjust as the change progresses and new information is gathered. The process for evaluating results as part of the monitoring phase for a program includes these steps:
Data collection	Data collection involves collecting data and information on the progress and effectiveness of the change program with data on KPIs, surveys and stakeholder interviews.
Data analysis	Collect and analyse data to evaluate the progress and effectiveness of the change program. This can include analysing the data in relation to the intended goals and objectives of the change program, identifying any issues or obstacles that have arisen, and determining if any adjustments or further actions are needed to the program.
Reporting	Create a report on the results of the monitoring phase. The report should include an overview of the progress and effectiveness of the change program, an analysis of the data collected, and recommendations for next steps. The report should be shared with stakeholders and relevant parties.
Decision-making	Use the information gathered in the monitoring phase to make informed decisions about the future direction of the change program. This can include deciding whether to continue with the change program as planned, make adjustments to the program, or terminate the program.
Action	Take the actions based on the previous decisions made
Continual monitoring	Continually monitor the progress and results of the program.

4.4 Results best practices

General overview	By following these best practices, firms can effectively evaluate the progress and effectiveness of their program and make informed decisions about its future direction.
Establish clear goals and objectives	Make sure to have clear and measurable goals and objectives for the change program to evaluate its progress.
Setting up KPIs	Establish KPIs can help to track progress and measure the success of the program. These KPIs should be specific, measurable, achievable, relevant, and time-bound (SMART).
Regular data collection and analysis	Regularly collect and analyse data on the progress of the program can help to identify issues & measure progress.
Involve stakeholders	Involving stakeholders in the monitoring process through surveys & interviews, can help to gather valuable feedback.
Communicate results effectively	Communicate the results of the monitoring phase effectively to stakeholders can help to maintain support and buy-in.
Continual monitoring	Continually monitoring the progress and results of the change program identifies any issues that arise& adjust as needed.
Continual learning	Continual learn from the monitoring phase can help to improve future change programs and the firm's capabilities.
Be Flexible	Be prepared to adjust the monitoring process as the change program progresses as new information is gathered.
Use a combination of methods	Use a combination of data collection methods as quantitative and qualitative methods, to get a well-rounded understanding of the change program's progress and effectiveness.

4.4 Results risks

General overview	By identifying and managing these risks, firms can ensure that they are effectively evaluating the progress and effectiveness of their change program and making informed decisions about its future direction.
Lack of data	Without proper data collection and analysis, it may be difficult to evaluate the progress of the change program making it difficult to identify issues & make informed decisions.
Inaccurate data	Poorly executed data collection methods can lead to unreliable data leading to incorrect conclusions about the progress and effectiveness of the change program.
Lack of stakeholder engagement	Without involving stakeholders in the monitoring process, it may be difficult to gather valuable feedback on the program leading to a lack of buy-in & support for the change program.
Lack of action	Without taking action based on the results of the monitoring phase, the change program may not progress or succeed.
Lack of flexibility	A rigid monitoring process that is not adapted to the program can lead to missing important information.
Resistance to change	Negative results may lead to resistance from stakeholders making it more difficult to execute the program.
Difficulty in comparing results	Without measurable goals, it may be difficult to compare results to the intended outcomes of the change program.
Limited resources	Without sufficient resources, it may be difficult to effectively monitor and evaluate the results of the change program.

4.4 Results lessons learned

General overview	By learning from these lessons, firms can improve their ability to evaluate the progress and effectiveness of their change programs, make informed decisions about their future direction, and ensure their success.
Clear and measurable goals and objectives	Having clear and measurable goals and objectives for the program can help to evaluate its progress and effectiveness.
The value of regular data collection	Regularly collect and analyse data on the progress and effectiveness of the change program can help to identify issues and measure progress towards goals.
Stakeholder engagement	Involve stakeholders in the monitoring process helps to gather valuable feedback on the change program.
Effective communication	Communicate the results of the monitoring phase effectively to stakeholders helps to maintain support for the program.
Continual monitoring	Continually monitor the progress and results of the program helps to identify any issues that arise & to adjust as needed.
Flexibility	Being flexible and adapting the monitoring process to the program helps to capture information & adjust as needed.
Learning from results	Learn from the monitoring phase helps to improve future change programs and the firm's change capabilities.
The need for proper resources	Having sufficient resources can be crucial for effectively monitoring and evaluating the results of the change program.

4.5 Improvement

The purpose of improvement during the monitoring phase of a change program is to ensure that the changes implemented are achieving the desired results and that any issues or problems are identified and addressed in a timely manner.

This includes evaluating the effectiveness of the changes, making any necessary adjustments, and continuously monitoring progress to ensure that the program stays on track and meets its goals.

By regularly assessing and improving the program, organizations can ensure that they are making the most effective use of resources and achieving the desired outcomes.

If improvement is not done as part of the monitoring phase for a change program, the negative impacts can include:

- Without regular assessment and improvement, the program may not be achieving its intended results or may be using resources in an inefficient manner.

- Without monitoring and improvement, the program may not be able to achieve its desired outcomes, leading to a lack of progress or even failure.
- It may be difficult to hold individuals accountable for their actions, leading to a lack of ownership and responsibility for the program.
- Without regular communication and progress updates, stakeholders may lose interest or confidence in the program, reducing support.
- Potential issues or opportunities may go unnoticed, leading to missed opportunities for growth or improvement.
- Unforeseen issues may arise that could have been prevented or addressed with earlier intervention.

Overall, without improvement as part of the monitoring phase, a change program may not achieve its intended results, and the organization may miss out on opportunities for growth and progress.

4.5 Improvement workstream activities

Reviews	**Review & analyse results.**
	Regularly review and analyse the results of the change program to identify areas for improvement.
Feedback	**Establish a feedback process.**
	Establish a process to capture and include feedback from stakeholders, team members, and other relevant parties.
Changes	**Identify changes based on results.**
	Identify and execute changes and improvements based on the results and feedback.
Progress	**Continuously monitor progress.**
	Continuously monitor progress against the program's objectives & metrics so that the improvements are effective.
Alignment	**Align processes to best practices.**
	Regularly evaluate and updating the program's processes to align with best practices & industry standards.
Improvement outcome	**Continual improvement.**
	Use the results of the monitoring and evaluation phase to identify opportunities for continual improvement of the change program and making adjustments as necessary.

4.5 Improvement questions

General overview	By regularly and systematically addressing these questions, firms can ensure that the program stays on track, addresses any issues that arise, and continuously improves its results.
Desired results	Are the changes achieving the desired results?
Issues from changes	Are there any issues that have arisen as a result of changes?
Changes execution	Are the changes being executed in an effective manner?
Opportunities	Are there any opportunities for extra program improvements?
Goals relevance	Are the program's goals and objectives still relevant?
Progress & status	Are all stakeholders aware of the progress & program status?
Potential risks	Are there any potential risks that need to be addressed?
Resource use	Are the allocated program resources being used effectively?
Program metrics	Are the program's metrics and key performance indicators (KPIs) being tracked and reported accurately?
Any other useful data required	Are there any additional data that would be useful for monitoring and improving the program?

4.5 Improvement process steps

General overview	It's important to mention that these steps should be done in a collaborative way with the involved stakeholders, to ensure that the solutions and adjustments are aligned with the objectives and goals of the change program.
Data collection	Collect data on program progress and performance using metrics, KPIs and other relevant information.
Analysis	Analyse the data to identify areas of success and areas for improvement.
Identification of issues	Identify any issues that have arisen as a result of the changes & prioritize them based on their impact and urgency.
Root cause analysis	Identify the root cause of any issues identified.
Solution development	Develop solutions or adjustments to address the identified issues and opportunities for improvement.
Implementation	Implement the solutions in a timely and effective manner.
Evaluation	Evaluate the effectiveness of the solutions or adjustments, and make any necessary adjustments.
Communication	Communicate progress and any issues to all stakeholders.
Continual monitoring	Continuously monitor program progress and performance.

4.5 Improvement best practices

General overview	By following these best practices, firms can ensure that their change program is on track, addressing any issues that arise, and continuously improving to achieve its intended results.
Clearly defined goals and metrics	Establish clear goals and metrics to measure progress and success of the program.
Regular monitoring	Schedule regular monitoring sessions to review progress, identify issues, and make adjustments as needed.
Collaborative approach	Engage all stakeholders and team members in the monitoring and improvement process to ensure buy-in and commitment.
Root cause analysis	Use root cause analysis to identify the underlying causes of issues, rather than just addressing symptoms.
Data-driven decisions	Use data to inform decisions and adjustments to the program.
Continuous improvement	Adopt a continuous improvement mindset, and continuously look for ways to improve the program.
Risk management	Identify and manage potential risks to the program, in order to proactively address them.
Communication	Regularly communicate progress, issues, and adjustments to all stakeholders and team members.
Flexibility	Be flexible and make adjustments to the program as needed.
Learning culture	Encourage a culture of learning, reflection, and continuous improvement within the organization.

4.5 Improvement risks

General overview	By being aware of these risks &proactively managing them, firms can ensure that their improvement process is effective
Lack of buy-in	If stakeholders do not fully understand or support the change program, they may be resistant to the improvement process, making it difficult to achieve desired results.
Limited resources	Limited resources such as time, budget and personnel may hinder the monitoring and improvement process.
Data quality	Poor quality data can lead to inaccurate conclusions, and incorrect decisions or actions.
Lack of standardization	Without standardization in the improvement process, it can be difficult to compare progress & performance across teams.
Resistance to change	Some individuals may resist change, making it difficult to implement new solutions or adjustments to the program.
Lack of ownership	Without clear ownership & accountability, it may be difficult for improvement tasks are completed in a timely, effective way.
Limited scope	The monitoring and improvement process may be too narrow in scope, missing key areas that need attention.
Limited expertise	Limited expertise in the specific domain of the change program may lead to poor decisions or ineffective solutions.
Lack of communication	Without proper comms, stakeholders may not be aware of progress or issues, making it difficult to address them.

4.5 Improvement lessons learned

General overview	It's important to document these lessons learned and share them across the firm, to leverage them for future programs.
Clearly defined goals	Clearly defined goals and metrics are essential for measuring progress and success.
Regular monitoring & improvement	Regular monitoring and improvement are crucial for identifying and addressing issues in a timely manner.
Collaborative approach	A collaborative approach that involves all stakeholders and team members is important for ensuring buy-in & support.
Root cause analysis	Root cause analysis is essential for identifying the underlying causes of issues and developing effective solutions.
Data-driven decisions	Data-driven decisions are important for making informed adjustments to the program.
Continuous improvement	Continuous improvement is a key mindset that helps organizations achieve desired results.
Risk management	Risk management is important for proactively addressing potential risks to the program.
Regular comms	Regular communication is essential for keeping all stakeholders and team members informed and engaged.
Flexibility	Flexibility is important for adapting to changing circumstances and making adjustments as needed.
A culture of learning	A culture of learning, reflection, and continuous improvement is essential for achieving long-term success.

YOUTH IS A BLUNDER; MANHOOD A STRUGGLE, OLD AGE A REGRET.

Benjamin Disraeli

5.0 Sustainable

The primary goal of the sustainability phase in a change management program is to ensure that the changes implemented during the program are embedded and sustained within the firm over time. This includes creating an environment that supports the new processes, systems, and behaviours, and making sure that the changes are fully integrated into the organization's culture and operations. The sustainability phase also includes providing ongoing support and training to the stakeholders, to ensure they have the necessary skills and knowledge to maintain the new changes. Additionally, this phase includes monitoring and measuring the performance to ensure that the changes are still delivering the intended benefits and making any necessary adjustments. The goal of this phase is to make sure that the changes implemented during the change management program become a permanent part of the firm and continue to deliver value over the long-term.

The 5 key components and associated activities for the sustainment phase for a change management program are the following:

1. Maintaining momentum of the change program to ensure that the benefits are sustained over time.
2. Embedding the change ensures the change is fully embedded in the organizational culture and processes, and that it is integrated into the day-to-day operations of the organization.
3. Continual improvement involves implementing a process for continual improvement so that the change program remains effective over time.
4. Communicating and celebrating ongoing success of the change program to stakeholders and celebrating ongoing achievements.
5. Sustaining the change involves identifying and implementing actions that will help the organization to sustain the change over the long term. This may include regular check-ins, reinforcing training, or creating incentives to maintain the change.

5.0 Sustainable Plan Linkages

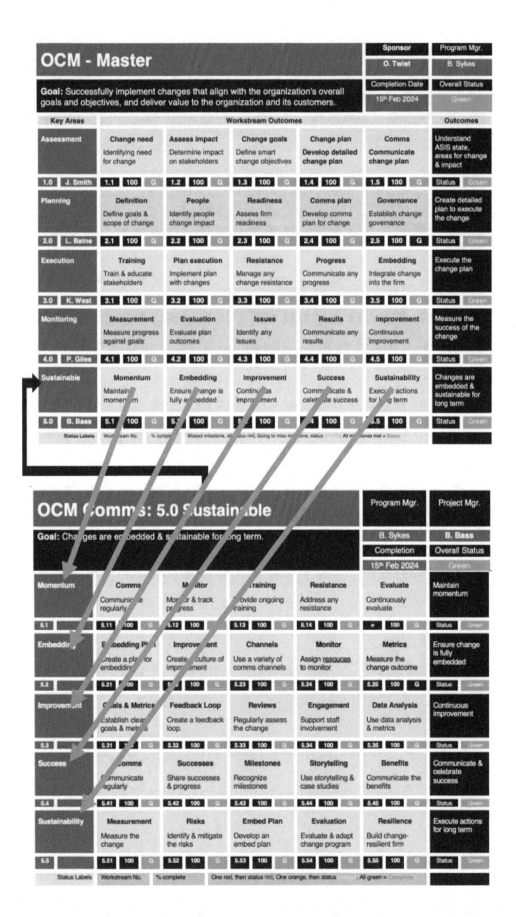

5.0 Sustainable Workstream Plan

OCM Comms: 5.0 Sustainable					Program Mgr.	Project Mgr.
					B. Sykes	**B. Bass**
Goal: Changes are embedded & sustainable for long term.					Completion	Overall Status
					15th Feb 2024	Green

Momentum	**Comms** Communicate regularly	**Monitor** Monitor & track progress	**Training** Provide ongoing training	**Resistance** Address any resistance	**Evaluate** Continuously evaluate	Maintain momentum
5.1	5.11 100 G	5.12 100 G	5.13 100 G	5.14 100 G	= 100 G	Status Green
Embedding	**Embedding Plan** Create a plan for embedding	**Improvement** Create a culture of improvement	**Channels** Use a variety of comms channels	**Monitor** Assign resources to monitor	**Metrics** Measure the change outcome	Ensure change is fully embedded
5.2	5.21 100 G	5.22 100 G	5.23 100 G	5.24 100 G	5.25 100 G	Status Green
Improvement	**Goals & Metrics** Establish clear goals & metrics	**Feedback Loop** Create a feedback loop.	**Reviews** Regularly assess the change	**Engagement** Support staff involvement	**Data Analysis** Use data analysis & metrics	Continuous improvement
5.3	5.31 100 G	5.32 100 G	5.33 100 G	5.34 100 G	5.35 100 G	Status Green
Success	**Comms** Communicate regularly	**Successes** Share successes & progress	**Milestones** Recognize milestones	**Storytelling** Use storytelling & case studies	**Benefits** Communicate the benefits	Communicate & celebrate success
5.4	5.41 100 G	5.42 100 G	5.43 100 G	5.44 100 G	5.45 100 G	Status Green
Sustainability	**Measurement** Measure the change	**Risks** Identify & mitigate the risks	**Embed Plan** Develop an embed plan	**Evaluation** Evaluate & adapt change program	**Resilience** Build change-resilient firm	Execute actions for long term
5.5	5.51 100 G	5.52 100 G	5.53 100 G	5.54 100 G	5.55 100 G	Status Green

Status Labels | Workstream No. | % complete | One red, then status red, One orange, then status , All green = Complete

5.1 Momentum

The purpose of momentum in the sustainable phase of a change program is to ensure that the changes implemented during the earlier phases of the program are maintained and continue to be effective over time.

The goals and objectives of momentum in this phase may include:

- Ensuring that the changes become deeply ingrained in the culture and practices of the organization
- Continuously monitoring and measuring the effectiveness of the changes
- Identifying and addressing any issues or obstacles that may arise during the sustainable phase
- Continuously communicating the benefits and progress of the changes to stakeholders
- Building a sense of ownership and commitment among employees to the changes
- Continuously improving and adapting the changes as necessary to meet the evolving needs of the firm.

Not maintaining momentum in the sustainable phase of a change program can have several negative impacts:

- Reversion to old habits and practices if the changes are not deeply ingrained in the culture and practices of the organization, employees may revert to their old ways of working, undoing the progress made during the earlier phases of the program.
- Without ongoing communication and progress updates, stakeholders may lose interest and support for the changes, making it more difficult to maintain them.
- Without ongoing monitoring and measurement, it can be difficult to identify and address any issues that arise during the sustainable phase.
- Decreased employee engagement without a sense of ownership and commitment among staff, they may be less likely to embrace the changes, which can negatively impact the success of the program.

5.1 Momentum workstream activities

Comms	**Communicate regularly.**
	Communicate regularly and effectively to all stakeholders to ensure they are aware of progress and any issues that arise.
Monitor	**Monitor & track progress.**
	Monitor and track progress against established goals and metrics to ensure the change program is on track.
Training	**Provide ongoing training.**
	Provide ongoing training & support to those impacted by the change to help them adjust and adopt new ways of working.
Resistance	**Address any resistance.**
	Address and resolve any resistance or obstacles that arise during the change process.
Evaluate	**Continuously evaluate.**
	Continuously evaluate and adapt the change program as needed to ensure it stays aligned with the organization's overall strategy and goals.
Momentum outcome	**Changes are embedded & sustainable for long term.**
	Maintain the momentum of the change program to ensure that the benefits are sustained over time.

5.1 Momentum questions

General overview	It is worth noting that these are general questions and other questions may arise to ensure the momentum is sustained and the change is embedded in the organization.
Embedding the change into the culture	How can we ensure that the changes become deeply ingrained in the culture and practices of the organization?
Continually monitor change effectiveness	How can we continuously monitor and measure the effectiveness of the changes?
Issues or obstacles in the sustain phase	How can we identify and address any issues or obstacles that may arise during the sustainable phase?
Continuously comm the change benefits	How can we continuously communicate the benefits and progress of the changes to stakeholders?
Sense of ownership	How can we build a sense of ownership among staff?
Continuously improve and adapt	How can we continuously improve and adapt the changes as necessary to meet the evolving needs of the organization?
The program ROI	How can we measure the ROI of the change program?
Resistance to change	How can we evaluate resistance and how to overcome it?
Sustainability metrics	How can we ensure the sustainability of the changes and what are the indicators of sustainability?
The next change	How can we prepare the firm for the next change?

5.1 Momentum plan components

General overview	It's important to note that these are general components and depending on the specific change program, other components may be necessary to ensure momentum is sustained and the change is embedded in the organization.
Communication plan	A communication plan that outlines how the organization will continue to communicate the benefits and progress of the changes to stakeholders (staff, stakeholders, third parties).
Training and development	A training and development plan to ensure that employees are equipped with the necessary skills and knowledge to successfully implement and maintain the changes.
Monitoring and measurement	A plan for ongoing monitoring and measurement of the changes to identify and address any issues or obstacles that may arise during the sustainable phase.
Continuous improvement	A plan for continuous improvement that outlines how the organization will continuously evaluate and adapt the changes as needed to meet the evolving needs of the firm.
Stakeholder engagement	A plan for engaging stakeholders, including employees, customers, and other relevant parties, to build a sense of ownership and commitment to the changes.
Resistance management	A plan to address any resistance to change, by identifying the reasons for resistance, evaluating their impact and implementing strategies to overcome it.
Sustainability	A plan to ensure the sustainability of the changes, by identifying the indicators of sustainability, measure them, and implement actions to maintain them.

5.1 Momentum best practices

General overview	It's important to note that these are general best practices & other best practices may be necessary to ensure momentum is sustained and the change is embedded in the organization.
Clear communication	Continuously communicate the benefits and progress of the changes to stakeholders so they are aware of how their roles and responsibilities have changed as a result of the program.
Employee engagement	Encourage staff to take an active role in the changes, and provide them with opportunities to provide feedback.
Continuous improvement	Continuously evaluate and adapt the changes to meet the evolving needs of the organization, and encourage employees to identify opportunities for improvement.
Monitoring and measurement	Continuously monitor the effectiveness of the changes, and use this information to make adjustments as needed.
Stakeholder engagement	Engage stakeholders to build a sense of ownership and commitment to the changes.
Resistance management	Address any resistance to change by identifying the reasons & evaluating their impact & executing actions to overcome it.
Sustainability	Identify the indicators of sustainability, measure them, and implement actions to maintain them.
Leadership support	Ensure that the leadership team fully supports the changes & communicates the benefits and progress to all the firm.
Recognition and rewards	Recognize and reward employees for their contributions to the change program, and celebrate successes along the way.

5.1 Momentum risks

Reversion to old habits and practices	If the changes are not deeply ingrained in the culture and practices of the firm, staffmay revert to their old ways of working, undoing the progress made so far in the program.
Loss of support	Without ongoing communication and progress updates, stakeholders may lose interest and support for the changes.
Decreased effectiveness	Without ongoing monitoring and measurement, it can be difficult to identify and address any issues that arise during the sustainable phase decreasing the change effectiveness.
Decreased employee engagement	Without a sense of ownership and commitment among staff, they may be less likely to fully embrace and support the changes, which can negatively impact the program success.
Missed opportunities for improvement	Without continuous improvement, the changes may become ineffective over time, which can lead to missed opportunities for making the firm more efficient, effective or profitable.
Lack of leadership support	If the leadership team does not fully support the changes, it can be hard to gain buy-in from staff to maintain momentum.
Limited resources	Limited resources (budget, human resources, or technology) can make it difficult to implement and maintain the changes, which can negatively impact the momentum of the program.
Overlooking key stakeholders	Not engaging or involving the right stakeholders (customers or external partners) can lead to missed opportunities, resistance, or lack of support for the change program.

5.1 Momentum lessons learned

Communication is key	Communicating the benefits and progress of the changes to stakeholders, including employees & customers is crucial for maintaining momentum and buy-in.
Employee engagement is important	Encouraging employees to take an active role in the changes and providing them with opportunities to provide feedback and suggestions for improvement can lead to a greater sense of ownership and commitment to the changes.
Continuous improvement is essential	Continuously evaluating and adapting the changes to meet the evolving needs of the organization, and encouraging employees to identify opportunities for improvement is important to ensure the changes remain effective over time.
Monitor and measure progress	Continuously monitoring and measuring the effectiveness of the changes, and using this information to make adjustments and improvements as needed is important to ensure the changes are meeting the desired outcomes.
Resistance management is necessary	Resistance to change is normal, and it's important to address it by identifying the reasons for resistance, evaluating their impact and implementing strategies to overcome it.

5.1 Momentum lessons learned

Sustainability is a must	Identifying the indicators of sustainability, measure them, and implement actions to maintain them is necessary to ensure the changes are lasting & have a positive impact on the firm
Prepare for the next step	Preparing the organization for the next change or innovation by creating a roadmap for future improvements and aligning it with the organization's overall strategy is important to ensure a continuous improvement mindset.
Leadership support is critical	Leadership support is critical for the success of any change program, it is important to ensure the leadership team fully supports the changes and actively communicates the benefits and progress to the rest of the organization.
Recognition and rewards are motivational	Recognizing and rewarding employees for their contributions to the change program, and celebrating successes along the way can help to maintain momentum and engagement.
Be flexible and adaptive	Change programs are dynamic, and it is key to be flexible & adaptive to the changing circumstances, so the momentum is sustained and the changes are embedded in the firm

5.2 Embedding

The purpose of embedding in the sustainable phase of a change program is to ensure that the changes implemented during the earlier phases of the program become a permanent part of the organization's culture, processes, and practices.

The goals and objectives of embedding in this phase may include:

- Ensuring that the changes are deeply ingrained in the culture and practices of the organization, so they are not easily undone or forgotten.
- Encouraging employees to take ownership of the changes and building a sense of commitment to them, so they continue to be supported in the long-term.
- Continuously measuring and monitoring the effectiveness of the changes to ensure they are meeting their intended goals and objectives.

- Addressing any resistance to the changes and implementing strategies to overcome it, so the changes can be fully embraced by employees.
- Continuously improving and adapting the changes as necessary to meet the evolving needs of the firm.
- Ensuring the changes are aligned with the organization's values, vision, and mission, and that they are supported by the leadership team and communicated effectively to the rest of the organization.
- Identifying the indicators of sustainability, measure them, and implement actions to maintain them.
- Preparing the organization for the next change or innovation by creating a roadmap for future improvements and aligning it with the organization's overall strategy.

Embedding the changes in the sustainable phase of the change program is crucial to ensure that the changes are lasting and have a positive impact on the organization.

5.2 Embedding workstream activities

Embedding Plan	Create a plan for embedding.
	Create a clear plan for embedding the change, including timelines, responsibilities, and metrics for success.
Improvement	Create a culture of improvement.
	Foster a culture of continuous improvement, encouraging employees to identify and implement new ways to improve processes and achieve goals.
Channels	Use a variety of comms channels.
	Use a variety of communication channels to educate and engage employees about the change, including face-to-face meetings, email updates, webinars, and training sessions.
Monitor	Assign resources to monitor.
	Assign dedicated resources to monitor and support the change, including change agents, coaches, and mentors.
Metrics	Measure the change outcome.
	Establish a system for monitoring and measuring the effectiveness of the change, and use the data to make adjustments and improvements as needed.
Embedding outcome	Ensure the change is fully embedded.
	Ensure the change is fully embedded in the firm's culture and processes, and that it is integrated into the day-to-day operations of the organization.

5.2 Embedding questions

General overview	During the sustain phase of a change program, key questions to consider when embedding the changes include:
Changes are integrated in processes	How can we ensure that the changes are fully integrated into the organization's processes and systems?
Maintain momentum	How can we maintain momentum and continue to drive adoption of the changes?
Metrics for ongoing effectiveness	How can we measure the ongoing effectiveness of the changes and make adjustments as needed?
A culture of continual improvement	How can we build a culture of continuous improvement to support sustained change?
Prepare for resistance of change	How can we prepare for and manage resistance to the changes to ensure they are fully adopted?
Make change sustainable	How can we ensure the change is sustainable in the long-term and will not revert back to the original state?
Leverage change for new opportunities	How can we leverage the changes to identify and pursue new opportunities for improvement?

5.2 Embedding process steps

General overview	The steps for the embedding process in the sustain phase of a change program can include:
Reinforcing the changes	Communicate the benefits of the changes and how they align with the organization's goals and values. Provide training and resources to support the changes and make sure they are fully integrated into the organization's processes & systems.
Measuring and monitoring progress	Establish metrics to measure the effectiveness of the changes and track progress over time. Use this data to adjust as needed so the changes are having the desired impact.
A culture of continual improvement	Encourage staff to identify & pursue new opportunities for improvement & make a habit of continuous learning.
Managing resistance	Prepare for and manage resistance to the changes by communicating effectively and addressing concerns and objections. Create a culture of open comms & feedback.
Sustaining the change	Develop a plan to ensure the changes are sustainable in the long-term, this includes but not limited to regular reviews, monitoring progress, and making adjustments as needed.
Leveraging the changes	Identify and pursue new opportunities for improvement and growth that have emerged as a result of the changes.
Communicating the Success	Share the success of the changes and the benefits that have been achieved with staff, stakeholders and other parties.

5.2 Embedding best practices

General overview	Best practices for embedding in the sustain phase are:
Communicating the benefits of the change	Clearly communicate the benefits of the changes and how they align with the organization's goals and values. This can help to build support and buy-in for the changes.
Providing training and resources	Provide employees with the training and resources they need to fully understand and implement the changes. This can include training on new processes, systems, and tools.
Measuring and monitoring progress	Establish metrics to measure the effectiveness of the changes and track progress over time. Use this data to adjust as needed so the changes are having the desired impact.
A culture of continual improvement	Encourage staff to identify and pursue new opportunities for improvement and make a habit of continuous learning.
Sustaining the change	Develop a plan to ensure the changes are sustainable in the long-term, this includes but not limited to regular reviews, monitoring progress, and making adjustments as needed.
Leveraging the changes	Identify and pursue new opportunities for improvement and growth that have emerged as a result of the changes.
Recognizing and rewarding success	Recognize and reward employees who have successfully adopted and implemented the changes. This can help to build momentum and encourage others to do the same.
Communicating the Success	Share the success of the changes and the benefits that have been achieved with employees, stakeholders, and parties.

5.2 Embedding risks

General overview	There are several risks that firm may face when embedding changes during the sustain phase of a change program:
Reversion to old ways	Without proper reinforcement and follow-up, employees may begin to revert back to their old ways of working, undoing the progress made during the change program.
Resistance to change	Employees may resist the changes and refuse to adopt them, which can slow down or even halt progress.
Lack of ownership	Without proper communication and buy-in, employees may not feel a sense of ownership over the changes, making it difficult to sustain them in the long-term.
Lack of measurement and monitoring	Without proper metrics in place to measure the effectiveness of the changes, it may be difficult to know if they are having the desired impact and make adjustments as needed.
Lack of a plan for sustainable change	Without a clear plan for ensuring the changes are sustainable in the long-term, it may be difficult to maintain progress and prevent reverting back to the original state.
Limited resources	Limited resources (budget & staff) may make it difficult to fully embed the changes so they are sustainable in the long-term.
Lack of leadership support	Without strong leadership support for the changes, it may be difficult to achieve buy-in and maintain momentum.
Lack of communication	Without clear and transparent comms, staff may not fully understand the changes and the reasons behind them, which can make it difficult to gain buy-in and achieve success.

5.2 Embedding lessons learned

Reinforcement and follow-up are crucial	To ensure the changes are fully embedded and sustainable, it is important to reinforce the changes and provide follow-up to ensure they are fully adopted and integrated into the organization's processes and systems.
Communication and buy-in are critical	Clear and transparent comms & buy-in from staff, are crucial for achieving success in the sustain phase of a program.
Metrics and monitoring are essential	Establishing metrics to measure the effectiveness of the changes and tracking progress over time is important to so changes have the desired impact and adjust as needed.
Culture of continual improvement	Build a culture of continuous improvement is important to so changes are sustainable in the long-term, and that new opportunities for improvement are identified and pursued.
Resistance to change should be expected	Resistance to change should be expected and addressed, by communicating effectively and addressing concerns.
Sustainability should be planned for	Have a plan to ensure changes are sustainable in the long-term is key to prevent reverting back to the original state.
Recognizing and rewarding success	Recognizing and rewarding employees who have successfully adopted and implemented the changes can help to build momentum and encourage others to do the same.
Communicating the success	Communicating the success of the changes and the benefits that have been achieved with staff and stakeholders can help to build support and buy-in for the changes.

5.3 Improvement

The purpose of improvement in the sustain phase of a change program is to ensure that the changes that were implemented during the earlier phases of the program (such as the planning and implementation phase) are fully integrated into the organization's processes and systems, and are being adopted and used by employees. The goal is to sustain the changes over time and ensure they continue to have a positive impact on the organization.

The specific goals of improvement in the sustain phase of a change program can include:

- Ensuring the changes are fully integrated into the organization's processes and systems which includes making sure that staff are trained on the changes, and that the resources and tools are there to support them.

- Maintaining momentum and continuing to drive adoption of the changes includes communicating the benefits of the changes and how they align with the organization's goals and values, and recognizing and rewarding employees who have successfully adopted and implemented the changes.

- Establishing metrics to measure the effectiveness of the changes and tracking progress over time is important to ensure the changes are having the desired impact and make adjustments as needed.

- Encouraging employees to identify and pursue new opportunities for improvement and make a habit of continuous learning and development.

- Preparing for and managing resistance to the changes by communicating effectively and addressing concerns and objections.

5.3 Improvement activities

Goals & metrics	**Establish clear goals and metrics.**
	Establish clear goals and metrics to measure the success of the change program and track progress over time.
Feedback loop	**Create a feedback loop.**
	Create a feedback loop to gather input from employees and stakeholders, and use this feedback to make adjustments and improvements to the change program.
Reviews	**Regularly assess the change.**
	Regularly review and assess the change program to identify areas for improvement, and implement changes as needed.
Engagement	**Support staff involvement.**
	Encourage and support employee involvement and empowerment in the continual improvement process.
Data analysis	**Use data analysis & metrics**
	Make use of data analysis and performance metrics to identify areas for improvement and make data-driven decisions for future changes.
Improvement outcome	**Continuous improvement.**
	Implement a process for continual improvement so that the change remains relevant &effective over time.

5.3 Improvement questions

General overview	Asking these questions, and being able to answer them, can help organizations to identify areas where improvements can be made and take action to sustain the changes over time.
Changes are integrated into firm's processes	How can we ensure that the changes are fully integrated into the organization's processes and systems?
Ongoing effectiveness metrics	How can we measure the ongoing effectiveness of the changes and make adjustments as needed?
Staff adoption	Are employees adopting and using the changes as intended?
Maintaining momentum	How can we maintain momentum and continue to drive adoption of the changes?
A culture of continual learning	How can we build a culture of continuous improvement to support sustained change?
Resistance of change	How can we prepare for and manage resistance to the changes to ensure they are fully adopted?
Ensure the change is sustainable	How can we ensure the change is sustainable in the long-term and will not revert back to the original state?
Leverage the change for new opportunities	How can we leverage the changes to identify and pursue new opportunities for improvement?
Delivering the desired results	Are the changes delivering the desired results and benefits to the organization and its stakeholders?
Changes are aligned with strategic goals	How can we ensure that the changes continue to be aligned with the organization's goals and objectives?

5.3 Improvement process steps

General overview	Implementing these steps can help organizations to identify areas where improvements can be made, take action to sustain the changes over time and make sure they are aligned with the organization's goals and objectives.
Measure and monitor progress	Establish metrics to measure the effectiveness of the changes and track progress over time. Use this data to adjust as needed so the changes are having the desired impact.
Identify areas for improvement	Use the data collected in step 1 to identify areas where improvements can be made and take action to address them.
Communicate progress and results	Share the progress and results of the changes with employees, stakeholders, and other key audiences. This can help to build support and buy-in for the changes.
Leverage the changes for new opportunities	Identify and pursue new opportunities for improvement and growth that have emerged as a result of the changes.
Continuously improve	Make a habit of continuous learning and encourage staff to identify and pursue new opportunities for improvement.
Ensure sustainability	Develop a plan to ensure the changes are sustainable in the long-term, this includes but not limited to regular reviews, monitoring progress, and making adjustments as needed.
Recognize and reward success	Recognize and reward employees who have successfully adopted and implemented the changes.
Communicating the Success	Share the success of the changes and the benefits that have been achieved with employees, stakeholders & other parties,

5.3 Improvement best practices

General overview	Implementing these best practices can help organizations to sustain the changes over time and make sure they are aligned with the organization's goals and objectives. Best practices for improvement in the sustain phase are:
Measuring and monitoring progress	Establish metrics to measure the effectiveness of the changes and track progress over time. Use this data to adjust as needed so the changes are having the desired impact.
Identifying areas for improvement	Use the data collected to identify areas where improvements can be made and take action to address them.
Communicating progress and results	Share the progress and results of the changes with employees, stakeholders, and other key audiences. This can help to build support and buy-in for the changes.
Ensuring sustainability	Develop a plan to ensure the changes are sustainable in the long-term, this includes but not limited to regular reviews, monitoring progress, and making adjustments as needed.
Aligning with firm's goals and objectives	Ensure the changes continue to be aligned with the organization's goals and objectives,& adjust as needed.
Involving staff in the improvement process	Involve employees in the improvement process and encourage them to share their ideas and feedback.

5.3 Improvement risks

General overview	here are several risks that organizations may face when it comes to improvement during the sustain phase are:
Lack of ownership	Without proper communication and buy-in, employees may not feel a sense of ownership over the changes, making it difficult to sustain them in the long-term.
Reversion to old ways	Without proper reinforcement and follow-up, employees may begin to revert back to their old ways of working, undoing the progress made during the change program.
Lack of leadership support	Without strong leadership support for the changes, it may be difficult to achieve buy-in and maintain momentum.
Lack of communication	Without clear and transparent comms, employees may not fully understand the changes and the reasons behind them, can make it difficult to gain buy-in and achieve success.
Lack of a plan for sustainable change	Without a clear plan for ensuring the changes are sustainable in the long-term, it may be difficult to maintain progress and prevent reverting back to the original state.
Unintended consequences	The changes may have unintended consequences, such as creating new problems among employees or stakeholders.
Lack of review and evaluation	Without regular review and evaluation of the progress and results of the changes, it may be difficult to know if they are having the desired impact and make adjustments as needed.

5.3 Improvement lessons learned

General overview	There are several key lessons that organizations can learn when it comes to improvement during the sustain phase are:
Reinforcement and follow-up are crucial	To ensure the changes are fully embedded and sustainable, it is important to reinforce the changes and provide follow-up to ensure they are fully adopted and integrated into the organization's processes and systems.
Involving employees in the improvement process	Involving employees in the improvement process and encouraging them to share their ideas and feedback can help to build buy-in and ownership of the changes.
Metrics and monitoring are essential	Establishing metrics to measure the effectiveness of the changes and tracking progress over time is important to ensure the changes are having the desired impact and make adjustments as needed.
Communication and buy-in are critical	Clear and transparent communication, as well as buy-in from employees, are crucial for achieving success in the sustain phase of a change program.
Communicating the Success	Sharing the success of the changes and the benefits that have been achieved with employees & stakeholders can help to build support and buy-in for the changes.

5.4 Success

The purpose of success activities in the sustain phase of a change program is to ensure that the changes that have been implemented are fully integrated into the organization's operations and culture, and that they continue to be supported and reinforced over time.

The goals of success activities in this phase include:

- Continuously monitoring and assessing the impact of the changes
- Identifying and addressing any issues or problems that arise
- Communicating the benefits of the changes to employees and stakeholders to reinforce their value
- Reinforcing the new behaviours, processes, and systems that have been introduced
- Building ownership and commitment among employees and stakeholders
- Continuously seeking feedback and making adjustments as needed to ensure the changes are effective and sustainable over time.

Success activities in the sustain phase can include things like ongoing training and coaching, regular progress reviews, and communication campaigns to reinforce the changes.

The overall goal is to make sure that the changes are fully embedded in the organization and that they continue to deliver value over time.

5.4 Success activities

Comms	**Communicate regularly.**
	Communicate regularly and effectively with all stakeholders to keep them informed of progress and any issues that arise.
Successes	**Share successes and progress.**
	Share successes & progress updates through various comms channels, including email, team meetings & town halls.
Milestones	**Recognize milestones.**
	Recognize and celebrate milestones and successes achieved as a result of the change program.
Storytelling	**Use storytelling and case studies.**
	Use storytelling and case studies to communicate the positive impact of the change program on the organization and its employees.
Benefits	**Communicate the benefits.**
	Continuously communicate the benefits and value of the change program to ensure buy-in and engagement from all stakeholders.
Success outcome	**Communicate & celebrate success.**
	Communicate the ongoing success of the change program to stakeholders and celebrating achievements along the way.

5.4 Success questions

General overview	The success activity in the sustain phase of a change program typically involves monitoring and evaluating the ongoing effectiveness of the changes that have been implemented. Questions that may be asked are:
Sustainable change	Are the changes being sustained over time?
Success metrics	What metrics are being used to measure change success?
Issues or challenges	Are there any issues or challenges that have arisen since the changes were implemented?
Additional improvements	Are there any additional improvements or adjustments that need to be made?
Feedback process	How is feedback from stakeholders being collected and used to improve the changes?
Steps to make changes permanent	What steps are being taken to ensure that the changes become a permanent part of the firm's culture &processes?
Change goals and objectives	Have the goals and objectives of the change program been met?

5.4 Success best practices

General overview	There are several best practices that can be used to celebrate success in a change program:
Recognize and reward individuals	Recognize and reward individuals and teams who have made significant contributions to the success of the program.
Share success stories	Share success stories and case studies with stakeholders to showcase the impact of the changes.
Communicate the results & benefits	Communicate the results and benefits of the program to all employees, stakeholders and customers to create a sense of pride and ownership.
Celebrate milestones	Celebrate milestones and achievements along the way to keep the team motivated and engaged.
Hold a formal celebration event,	Hold a formal celebration event, such as a reception or dinner, to bring everyone together and recognize the collective effort and success.
Communicate the success	Communicate the success of the program to external staff and stakeholders to demonstrate the firm's commitment to continuous improvement.
Communicate the impact of the change	Communicate the impact of the change program to the management and leadership of the organization, to showcase the benefits and return on investment.
Create a sense of continuity	Create a sense of continuity by planning for the next phase of the change program, and incorporating the lessons learned in the process.

5.5 Sustainability

The purpose of the sustainability phase in a strategic organization change management program is to ensure that the changes that have been implemented are fully integrated into the organization's operations and culture, and will be sustained over the long term.

The objectives of the sustainability phase typically include:

- Ensuring that the changes are fully embedded in the organization's processes, systems, and culture
- Identifying and addressing any remaining resistance to the change
- Establishing a plan to maintain and improve upon the changes over time
- Measuring and tracking progress against the established goals and objectives of the change initiative
- Identifying and addressing any issues that may arise in the future

The goals of the sustainability phase include:

- Ensuring that the changes become part of the organization's routine and culture
- Embedding the change into the organization's DNA
- Achieving a long-term positive impact on the organization's performance
- Continuously monitoring progress to ensure the change initiative is on track and achieving the desired outcomes
- Continuously improving the change initiative to meet the evolving needs of the organization.

In summary, the sustainability phase is the final step in a change management program and its goal is to ensure that the change is fully integrated and sustained within the organization to achieve a long-term positive impact.

5.5 Sustainability workstream activities

Measurement	**Measure the change.**
	Establish a system for monitoring and measuring the effectiveness of the change, and use the data to make adjustments and improvements as needed.
Risks	**Identify and mitigate risks.**
	Identify and mitigate potential risks that may arise during the implementation and sustainment of the change.
Embed plan	**Develop an embed plan.**
	Develop a plan to embed the change into the organization's culture and processes to ensure long-term adoption.
Evaluation	**Evaluate & adapt change program.**
	Continuously evaluate and adapt the change program as needed so it stays aligned with the firm's overall strategy.
Resilience	**Build change-resilient firm.**
	Build a change-resilient firm by providing ongoing training, support, and resources to employees to help them adapt and sustain the change over the long term.
Sustainability outcome	**Execute actions for long term.**
	Identify and implement actions that will help the firm to sustain the change over the long term with regular check-ins, reinforcing training, incentives to maintain the change.

5.5 Sustainability questions

General overview	The sustainability phase of a change program typically involves ensuring that the changes that have been implemented are fully integrated into the organization's culture and processes, and that they continue to deliver desired results over time.
Sustainable change	Are the changes being sustained over time?
Success metrics	What metrics being used to measure the change success?
Any change issues	Are there any issues arisen since the changes made?
More improvements	Are there any more improvements that need to be made?
Feedback process	How is feedback being collected and used to improve?
Steps to make change permanent	What steps are being taken so the changes become a permanent part of the organization's culture and processes?
Change goals met?	Have the goals of the change program been met?
Program comms	How is the program being communicated to the firm?
Leadership support	How is the change program being supported by leadership?
Program success celebration	Are there any plans to celebrate and acknowledge the success of the change program?

5.5 Sustainability plan components

General overview	A sustainable plan in the sustainability phase of a change program should include several key components in order to ensure that the changes are fully integrated into the organization's culture and processes, and that they continue to deliver desired results over time.
Measuring and monitoring	Establish a system for measuring and monitoring the progress and effectiveness of the changes, and using that data to make any necessary adjustments.
Communication and engagement	Develop a communication plan to keep stakeholders informed and engaged in the change program, and seeking feedback to improve the changes.
Leadership and accountability	Ensure that leadership is committed to the program and that there is accountability for achieving the desired results.
Training and development	Providing training and development to help employees understand and implement the changes, and to develop the necessary skills to sustain the changes.

5.5 Sustainability plan components

Reinforcement and rewards	Developing strategies to reinforce the changes and reward employees who embrace and support the changes.
Continuous improvement	Establishing a process for continuous improvement to identify and address any issues or challenges that arise, and to make ongoing improvements to the changes.
Embedding the changes	Include the changes into the firm's culture and processes so they become a permanent part of the way the firm operates.
Continuity plan	Having a plan in place to handle any unforeseen issues that may arise and to keep the change program on track.
Celebrating success	Acknowledging and celebrating the success of the change program to reinforce the changes and to promote a positive culture of change.

5.5 Sustainability best practices

General overview	Best practices for sustainability in the sustainability phase of a change program can include:
Continual monitoring	Continuously monitor and measurie the progress and effectiveness of the changes identifies any issues that arise and make adjustments as needed.
Engagement with stakeholders	Communicating and engaging with stakeholders ensures they are informed, understand the changes and are able to provide feedback on the changes.
Ongoing training & development	Providing ongoing training helps employees understand and implement the changes, and develop the necessary skills to sustain the changes.
Reinforcing changes with rewards	Reinforcing the changes through rewards and recognition ensures staff embrace the changes.
Continuously seeking opportunities	Continuously seeking opportunities for improvement identifies and addresses any issues that arise and make ongoing improvements to the changes.
Accountable leadership team	Having a leadership team that is fully committed and accountable for the program so the changes are fully supported and desired results are achieved.
Celebrating success	Celebrating the success to reinforce the changes and to promote a positive culture of change.
Building a culture of continuous improvement	Incorporating the mindset and practices of continuous improvement in the organization to ensure that the change program is not a one-time event, but rather a part of the organization's DNA.

5.5 Sustainability risks

General overview	There are several risks that can impact the sustainability of a change program during the sustainability phase, including:
Lack of ongoing support from leadership	If leadership does not continue to support and champion the changes, it can lead to resistance from employees and a lack of commitment to sustain the changes.
Insufficient monitoring and measurement	Without ongoing monitoring and measurement, it can be difficult to identify issues that arise and adjust as needed.
Inadequate comms and engagement	Without effective communication and engagement, it can be difficult to keep stakeholders informed and engaged, and to obtain feedback that can improve the changes.
Inadequate training and development	Without proper training, staff may not have the necessary skills and knowledge to implement and sustain the changes.
Lack of reinforcement and rewards	Without strategies to reinforce the changes and reward employees who embrace and support the changes, it can be difficult to sustain the changes.
Unforeseen issues	Unforeseen issues as internal disruptions may arise, which can impact the sustainability of the change program.
Lack of a continuity plan	Without a plan to handle any unforeseen issues that may arise, it can be difficult to keep the change program on track.
Failure to embed the changes	If the changes are not fully embedded into the organization's culture and processes, it can be difficult to make the changes a permanent part of the way the organization operates.

5.5 Sustainability lessons learned

General overview	The sustainability phase of a change program is focused on ensuring that the changes implemented during the program continue to be effective and efficient over the long-term. Some lessons that can be learned during this phase include:
Continuously monitor	Continuously monitor and evaluate the progress of the changes to ensure they are having the desired impact.
Communicate regularly	Communicate regularly with stakeholders to ensure that their needs and concerns are being addressed.
Plan for changes	Develop a plan for maintaining and updating the changes to ensure they remain relevant and effective.
Sustainability roadblocks	Identify and address any roadblocks to sustainability, such as a lack of resources or resistance from employees.
Changes are embedded into firm	Ensure that the changes are embedded into the firm's culture and processes to ensure they are sustained over time.
Continual improvement	Continuously strive for improvement and innovation to ensure the changes remain effective and efficient.

IT DOES NOT MATTER HOW SLOWLY YOU GO
AS LONG AS YOU DO NOT STOP.

Confucius

Acknowledgements

One Page Concept: Ken Martin

Source of Royalty Free Quotes (pre-1923):
The GoldenQuotes.Net

3 Magic Publications

Birmingham.

United Kingdom

3 Magic Publications

After an extensive successful career working for some of the best organisations in the world in various countries, I was disheartened to see how many times programs and projects failed from not paying heed to lessons learned and best practices. Even today, how many current programs are being executed without proper assessment, planning or organisational change management, And then organisations are surprised why so many of the programs and projects fail to deliver any business benefits.

I decided to author and to create several Best Practice Books based on my **One Page Magic**™ format on topics such as PMO, Project Management & Business Transformation for leaders to learn from other's experience for project success. When opportunities arise, I collaborate with others to capture their knowledge, experience and best practices to produce additional best practices books.

Other Publications on Amazon

OPM best practices handbooks
- PMO handbook
- Transformation handbook
- Transformational leadership handbook
- CIO handbook
- CTO handbook

One Page Magic series
- PMO magic
- Transformation magic
- PM magic
- Opex magic
- Leader magic
- Agile magic
- Career magic

The OPM 8-minute series
- CIO/ CTO guide
- DT/ CX guide
- Agile guide
- PMO setup guide
- Live your future guide
- Career guide
- Program planning guide
- Operational excellence guide
- Leadership guide
- Fintech guide
- Disruptive tech guide
- Transformation PMO guide
- PMO governance guide

The Magic Megabook series
- The transformation magic megabook
- The PMO magic megabook

Printed in Great Britain
by Amazon